Our Chawton home, how much we
    find
Already in it, to our mind;
And how convinced, that when
    complete
It will all other houses beat
That ever have been made or mended,
With rooms concise, or rooms
    distended . . .
                     Jane Austen

LIVING WITH OLD HOUSES

A PUBLICATION OF
THE ADVISORY SERVICE
OF GREATER PORTLAND LANDMARKS

Consulting Editors   JUDITH D. PARKER
PATRICIA McGRAW ANDERSON
GRACE TRAPPAN
ANNE P. HAZZARD

Graphics   SHIRLEY M. GEORGE
DORRY FRENCH
RUTH TRAPPAN
MARY-ELIZA WENGREN

Resource Library   IRIS ALMY

This book is dedicated to the
proud owners of old houses

CONTENTS

FOREWORD

The Advisory Service of Greater Portland Landmarks, Inc. developed with the organization's growth. Landmarks' initial Daniel How House (1799) restoration project involved a number of volunteers in doing research and learning restoration techniques. With the advice of the Consultant Bureau of the Providence Preservation Society, these volunteer researchers formed the Advisory Service to help old house owners. The collection of written and visual material increased and was deposited in Landmarks' Resource Center.

Although each Advisory Service member has some knowledge of the various facets of preservation and restoration, the tendency is to specialize in an area of personal interest and experience. Through the use of Landmarks' Resource Center, public libraries, and personal collections of books, articles, catalogues, photographs and other material, the members continue to become better informed. Much has been learned by talking to the curators at restoration centers such as Strawbery Banke in Portsmouth and Old Sturbridge Village where professional methods and techniques have been studied. Symposiums and lectures on restoration are attended for further study.

The Advisory Service conducts workshops which are open to the public. These workshops feature exhibits, demonstrations and talks on photographing and measuring old woodwork and hardware, uncovering old paint and reproducing old colors, the proper treatment of floors, mantels, fireplaces and chimneys, using lighting devices, and choosing fabrics and wallpapers appropriate to a period. The Advisory Service has a portable exhibit which can be set up in small spaces, lobbies or entrance halls.

Research continues. Studies are being made of special architectural features in the Greater Portland area. Pictures and measurements of front doors, mantels, stairways and other interior details of each architectural style are being assembled in notebooks and will be placed in the Resource Center for reference. If an owner wishes to restore a fireplace appropriate to the style of his house, for instance, these notebooks will provide a variety of possible choices. If architects, architectural historians or students need this specialized information, the notebooks will provide a unique source for them.

Please call the office of Greater Portland Landmarks for more information, and help expand the service by sharing knowledge acquired through your experience! More local examples and information are constantly being sought.

Frances Peabody
Dorrie Foss

PREFACE

The first edition of "Some Notes on Living with Old Houses" was a pocketed folder of mimeographed "notes" put together in response to questions asked of Greater Portland Landmarks' Advisory Service. This informal publication was such a success that in June of 1974 a book was printed which was greatly expanded in subjects, information, and bibliographies. By Christmas it was necessary to order reprints. The need for a new edition was apparent so the Advisory Service members decided to improve and revise their two earlier efforts.

The title of this edition, which has more subjects, line drawings, and a glossary, has been changed to **Living with Old Houses.** The intent of the book is the same. It is written for the new possessor of an old house, and for the more experienced home owner. The writers hope to help the reader to recognize architectural styles, to outline the first steps in planning restoration, and to indicate in more detail how to answer questions that will arise. Finally, the book aims to inspire in the reader the desire to become involved in the excitement of research and further reading through the use of the annotated bibliographies.

For their encouragement and helpful criticism, the Advisory Service wishes to thank the Society for the Preservation of New England Antiquities in Boston. We also acknowledge with gratitude the comments and ideas of Mr. Robert Mack of the Office of Archeology and Historical Preservation of the National Park Service.

EXPLANATORY NOTES

The list of abbreviations:

AASLH - American Association for State and Local History
APT - Association for Preservation Technology
GPL - Greater Portland Landmarks
PPL - Portland Public Library
R before call number - Reference book to be used in Library
LL - Local Library
SPNEA - Society for Preservation of New England Antiquities
OTNE - Old Time New England
MHS - Maine Historical Society
CCC - Cumberland County Courthouse
TO - Town Office

Notes on using the Bibliography in each section

a. If your local library does not own a certain title, it probably can borrow it on interlibrary loan from another library.

b. The Portland Public Library owns complete files of both Antiques Magazine and Old Time New England.

c. Numbers following "Portland Public Library" after a title are the Portland Public Library call number for that title.

d. Greater Portland Landmarks, Inc. owns complete files of both APT Bulletin and Old House Journal.

PRESERVATION, RESTORATION, RENOVATION AND CARE

Generally speaking it is better to preserve than repair, better to repair than restore, better to restore than reconstruct.

PRESERVATION means keeping an old building in good condition in its existing form.

RESTORATION means returning a building to some specific date (often the date it was supposedly built), replacing all changes made after that date with copies of what has been destroyed, and removing all work of a later period. This necessitates the use of new materials from other old buildings.

Charles E. Peterson's graphic phrase for this is "to early up a building." This really is a fanciful procedure and should be regarded as such. Change is part of the natural life of buildings and only increases their interest as antiquities.

RENOVATING (remodeling or rehabilitation) makes selective use of any changes in structure and detail, leaving those features which may make the building more adaptable to modern use.

1

RECONSTRUCTION means a recreation of a building from historical or architectural documents and other evidence often of a highly conjectural nature.

Any of these approaches may be appropriate. This is your house and it must be adapted to your living needs. THINK BEFORE YOU DESTROY.

Start with an overall plan: Any changes you make should be reversible by future owners - the slow, careful, well planned approach can save money and many regrets later. You may not be able to achieve all of your plan for many years, but it will save the expensive redoing of the results of impetuous early actions. Do a few things well and be content with seemingly slow progress. You will be more satisfied later.

Keep records right from the beginning. Photograph and measure each feature before you change anything. If possible, mark new material used in the house with the date on the back. (See "Making Plans and Keeping Records")

Learn all you can about your house. Research its age, its former occupants, its style of architecture. Most buildings have features in common with other buildings, often in the same neighborhood. Some details missing in yours may have survived elsewhere.

Study its structure, how it was built, which parts appear to be original and when the different additions were made. This may, in turn, suggest the best methods of adapting the house to your family's needs, while preserving its essential character.

Expert advice at this stage will prove very worthwhile later. If possible, before signing papers, a contractor should assess the structural repairs needed so this substantial and essential expense can be planned for in the original financing. Sills should be suspected of needing repair, until proven sound.

Heating, plumbing, electricity, while presenting real problems, need not be obtrusive if the installation is carefully planned and WATCHED AT EVERY STEP. Don't let anyone hack through main timbers or fine woodwork. Electric outlets can be set into the plaster where they barely show.

Electric wiring is rarely adequate or safe and should be redone. Ample outlets for lamps could obviate the necessity for ceiling fixtures; careful planning at this stage is a real money saver and will insure against fire hazards.

Ceilings: Hewn beams were rarely intended to be left exposed in houses after c. 1730 and even these early timbers were carefully smoothed and finished with chamfered edges. Another reason for not exposing the beams is the difficulty

2

of concealing the plumbing that often runs between them. Original plaster ceilings and walls should be saved and repaired if at all possible. Even if they are sagging badly, they can be attached to the lath with "plaster buttons", and holes and cracks can be patched. The natural slight undulations of an old ceiling are an essential part of an early house. The ornamental plaster ceilings and stamped metal ceilings and cornice mouldings of the Victorian period should also be retained and can add greatly to the interest of the room. (Material on this is available at the GPL Resource Center).

Most woodwork and floors were painted. Floors were usually covered. If you are lucky enough to have wide pine floors, try to avoid machine sanding, as this removes all their character. There are other solutions. Woodwork should be left painted; there are many good early colors available. Fine mouldings lose their intended effect when obscured by innumerable layers of paint, or when stripped and the wood left bare.

A search in the attic, cellar and outbuildings will often turn up discarded parts: old doors with original hardware, whose measurements indicate their original location before the advent of central heating; pieces of old mouldings; original window sash with small panes, indicating what windows the house used to have before large panes became popular.

Fashions in restoration change. There is no one 'right' way of doing anything. Professional preservationists change their opinions in the light of later research. The purpose of our suggestions in this book is to encourage the individual to become more aware of the potentialities of his house, to take time to do his own research and to think carefully before taking any steps that are irreversible.

BIBLIOGRAPHY

Bullock, Orin M. **The Restoration Manual: An Illustrated Guide to the Preservation and Restoration of Old Buildings.** Norwalk, Conn., Silvermine Publishers, 1966.
Available - GPL
Outlines procedures for authentic restoration of a variety of building types.

Dietz, Albert G. **Dwelling House Construction.** Princeton, N.J., Van Nostrand, 1946. Revised edition, Cambridge, Mass., M.I.T. Press, 1971.
Available - GPL
- PPL 690 D56 1954, 1971.
Details of construction - modern building specifications. An invaluable handbook on methods and materials.

Harvey, John **Conservation of Buildings.** London, John Baker, 1972. Toronto, Univ. of Toronto Press, 1972.
Available - GPL
"What to save - how to save it; craftsmanship and materials; continuing conservation" - illustrated with photographs of work in progress.

Insall, Donald W. **The Care of Old Buildings Today: A Practical Guide.** London, Architectural Press, 1972. N.Y., Watson Guptill Pub., 1974.
Available - GPL
Although this book is geared towards English conservation problems, it has much invaluable, relevant information on preservation theory and methods.

Judd, Henry A. **Before Restoration Begins - Keeping Your Historic House Intact.** History News, Vol. 28 no. 10. Technical leaflet no. 67 AASLH, 1973.
Investigate carefully before you start work.

McKee, Harley J. **Introduction to Early American Masonry: Stone, Brick, Mortar and Plaster.** Washington, D.C., National Trust, Columbia Univ., 1973.
Available - GPL

Phillips, Morgan **Philosophy of Preservation and Conservation.** (in APT, v. III no. 1, 1971, pp. 38-43.)
"Philosophy of Total Preservation." A recent statement of SPNEA policy.

Stephen, George **Remodeling Old Houses Without Destroying Their Character.** New York, Knopf, 1972.
Available - GPL
- PPL 728 S828

Williams, Henry L. and Ottalie. **Old American Houses 1700-1850, How to Restore, Remodel and Reproduce Them.**, N.Y., Bonanza, 1957.
Available - GPL
Basic book on construction methods and building types. A good book for any owner of an old house to have and to study before going on to others.

PERIODICALS

COMPLETE FILES PPL:

Antiques V.1, 1922-date R050 A63 Art

Old Time New England, the Bulletin of the Society for the Preservation of New England Antiquities V.1, July 1910-date R974 S67 Art.

COMPLETE FILES GPL:

Association for Preservation Technology 1969-date. *Quarterly.*

Old House Journal Jan. 1973-date. *Frequent valuable articles, well illustrated.*

Note:
The National Park Service is currently working on a comprehensive technical handbook dealing with "Professional methods and techniques for preserving, restoring and maintaining historic properties". When published, this will be an invaluable reference source. It will be published initially in segments in professional journals.

Old House Journal is publishing a list of specific restoration resource addresses this fall.
Historical Mineral Point Inc. has an excellent restoration list of resources available. 224 Clowney Street, Mineral Point, Wisc. 53565.

A PRIMER OF ARCHITECTURAL STYLES IN GREATER PORTLAND, MAINE

Few houses that we see today retain their original appearance. This is especially true of the earliest examples which have survived the greatest number of changes. Succeeding generations built according to the current fashion, giving us the rich variety of architectural style seen in Greater Portland Communities today.

Much can be learned of a town's development and economic life from looking at its buildings. A preponderance of one particular architectural style indicates a prosperous community at the time that style was popular. The survival of a number of early houses, perhaps camouflaged by later utilitarian siding, may indicate when depression hit the area after industry or population moved away, resulting in the construction of fewer new buildings.

One house may show evidence of many different architectural styles. Doorways, windows, and chimneys were frequently updated. Newer ells were added to houses; or newer, bigger houses were added to older ones which then became ells. (Because change is a natural process in the life of a house, any decision to remove later additions, in the name of restoration, should be approached with caution.) Also, a house may be transitional in character, combining elements of an established older architectural style with those of a newer style.

To attempt to precisely date a house by its architectural style is difficult and sometimes misleading. Geographical as well as socio-economic factors influenced the style in which a house was built; so did the age and the taste of the owner and his workmen. A high-style house whose owners were influenced by European fashion and architectural writings could have been built several generations ahead of a similar house in a more remote community. Change in style filtered down slowly and unevenly to the simple farmhouses.

Bearing these factors in mind, here are examples of some of the architectural styles frequently seen in the Greater Portland area and the approximate dates their appearance would suggest. The actual date of construction can only be established after much local research. Those features most typical of a style are listed. A single house is unlikely to show all the features of one style, but it will show some of them.

COLONIAL OR GEORGIAN STYLE   1750-1820

Look for: Plain, square appearance.   Buildings hugging the ground.
Huge central chimney.
Small paned windows close under narrow eaves.
Simple, narrow trim.
No blinds (shutters).
Simple, narrow doorway, often with transom lights over door, framed
 by classical mouldings.

FEDERAL STYLE   1780-1830

Look for: Symmetrical appearance with flat, horizontal lines.
Two or four chimneys in gable end walls or set in from gable ends.
Two chimneys on rear wall of narrow house. Some center chimneys persisting.
Windows usually spaced evenly, with blinds.
Occasional Palladian windows.
Delicate classical trim on windows and cornices.
Elaborate fan doorways, with sidelights.
Occasional hip roofs.
Frequent brick construction.
Three story buildings with four chimneys in towns.

GREEK REVIVAL STYLE   1830-1870

Look for: Heavy, blocky effect, even on small houses.
Pedimented "temple" effect.
Walls constructed to resemble smoothness of stone.
Thinner chimneys in various positions.
Larger windows and windowpanes, with blinds.
Trim of wide corner pilasters, often with recessed center panels.
Wide cornice with overhanging eaves.
Doorway framed by wide lintel and pilasters, usually with full-length
sidelights.
Gable end often toward street with doorway off center.

The VICTORIAN PERIOD lasted from 1837 to 1910, with English styles still influencing American architecture. The period covers a great diversity of styles, each with its own name and characteristics. Unlike the preceding square styles, which were all governed by the dictates of the heavy hewn braced-frame construction, house plans could now become increasingly complex due to the new, light balloon framing methods. Huge chimneys gave way to small stove chimneys which appeared through the roof in any number of places. Frequently during the late VICTORIAN PERIOD several styles would be combined in one architectural design. These are some of the styles more commonly seen in this area:

GOTHIC REVIVAL STYLE   1840-1880

Look for: Vertical, pointed effect.

Steeply pitched roof, often originally covered with slate or "tin".

Pointed gables and dormer windows.

Bay windows and porches.

Fancy, scrolled, machine-cut trim on gables, windows, porches, and eaves.

Vertical board siding, or simulated stone effect with matched boarding.

Thin, elaborate chimneys.

ITALIANATE STYLE   1840-1880

Look for: Massive, elaborate effect.

Flattish roofs. Roofs with wide overhanging eaves supported by heavy brackets.

Porches, bay windows, cupolas, balconies.

Arched or round window tops. Large windowpanes.

Heavy trim on doorways, cornice, cornerboards, and windows.

Massive doorways. Raised porch with steps.

Frequent double doors, sometimes with round tops, sometimes with etched glass.

MANSARD STYLE   1860-1890

Look for: Heavy roof coming down over side walls.
Bold three-dimensional effect.
Dormer windows protruding from steep curve of double pitched roof.
Overhanging eaves with brackets.
Bay windows and porches.
Several chimneys.
Elaborate wood or iron trim.
Entrances with double doors.
Porches with steps and balustrade.

STICK STYLE   1860-1910

Look for: Diagonal, vertical, and horizontal stickwork in trim, balconies, and
porches.
High, steep roof.
Projecting eaves supported by exposed framing in gable end.
Many spindly chimneys.
Extensive porches with roofs supported by columns with diagonal
braces.

QUEEN ANNE STYLE   1870-1910

Look for: Irregular layout with complex rooflines, turrets, and gables.
Variety of siding materials and textures.
Geometrically patterned windows of various shapes.
Bay windows, balconies, and porches giving three-dimensional effect.
Small, elaborate detail.
Tall, rectangular chimneys with decorative details.

12

SHINGLE STYLE   1880-1930

Look for: Flowing, complex shape unified by large roof.   Horizontal effect.
Walls as well as roof covered with shingles.
Towers, balconies, porches which create an interpenetration of exterior and interior space.
Natural stone foundations.
Massive rectangular chimneys.
Frequent gambrel roofs.

COLONIAL REVIVAL STYLE   1880-1930

A desire to bring back features of previous styles developed with the Shingle Style. The COLONIAL REVIVAL STYLE incorporated elements of the Colonial or Georgian Style and the Federal Style in elaborate houses. Sometimes elements of the COLONIAL REVIVAL STYLE were combined with those of the Shingle Style. Palladian windows, quoined cornerboards, hip roofs, and dormer windows are frequent features.

"PLAIN STYLE" 1750-on

In all periods some houses were so simply built by their owners, or were so altered, as to have no discernible stylistic trim.   Nevertheless, there are usually some details of shape or plan, or some window details, that can give a clue to the style of the house when compared with other houses in that area.

Text: Ursula Baier, Mary-Eliza Wengren.
Photographs: Shirley George, Freeport Historic Preservation Survey (17), Yarmouth Historic Preservation Survey (13, 24, 25), David Higgins (26), Gordon Smith (19, 20, 27).

BIBLIOGRAPHY

Chamberlain, Narcissa **Old Rooms for New Living; Being a Collection of Early American Interiors Authentic in Design, Various in Period, and Suitable for Today's Living.** New York, Hastings House, 1953. 2nd printing 1965.
Available - GPL

Cummings, Abbott Lowell **Architecture in Early New England,** Sturbridge, Mass., Old Sturbridge Inc., 1958. Revised Edition, 1974.
Available - GPL
- PPL 720.9744 C97
Brief survey of styles to mid-nineteenth century.

Downing, Andrew Jackson **Architecture of Country Houses, including Designs for Cottages and Farm-houses, and Villas, with Remarks on Interiors, Furniture, and the Best Modes of Warming and Ventilating** . . . New York, Appleton, 1850, New York, Dover reprint, 1969.
Available - GPL
- PPL 749 F852

Downing, Antoinette and Scully, Vincent **Architectural Heritage of Newport, R.I. 1640-1915.** Cambridge, Mass., Harvard Press, 1952, revised edition, N.Y., Clarkson Potter, 1967.
Available - GPL
Relevant examples of New England architecture in both photographs and drawings. Particularly useful for the later periods.

Greater Portland Landmarks **Portland.** Portland, Me. GPL Inc., 1972.
Available - GPL
- PPL 720.974194 qP582
Excellent illustrations show local building types and text describes them.

Hamlin, Talbot **Greek Revival Architecture in America; Being an Account of Important Trends in American Architecture and American Life prior to the War Between the States.** New York, Oxford Univ. Press, 1944. New York, Dover reprint, 1964.
Available - GPL
- PPL 724 H22
Origins and widespread examples of architectural styles in the Victorian period.

Howells, John Mead **Architectural Heritage of the Piscataqua; Houses and Gardens of the Portsmouth District of Maine and New Hampshire.** New York, Architectural Book Pub., Inc. 1937, 1965.
Available - GPL 1965 reprint
- PPL 1937 ed. R728 qH85

Isham, Norman M. and Mercer, Henry C. **Illustrated Glossary of Colonial Architecture and the Dating of Old Houses,** ed. by Hugh Guthrie. Century House.
Available - GPL
- PPL 728 I79

Kelly, J. Frederick **Early Domestic Architecture of Connecticut.** New Haven, Yale University Press, 1924. New York, Dover reprint, 1963.
Available - GPL Dover reprint
- PPL 1924 Edition R728 qK29
Excellent scale drawings of early houses, their details and construction.

Kettel, Russell Hawes, ed. **Early American Rooms: A Consideration of the Changes in Style.** Portland, Me., Southworth Press, 1936. New York, Dover reprint, 1967.
Available - GPL Dover reprint
- PPL 1936 ed. R747 qK43 Southworth
Useful for interior style changes. Excellent detailed drawings to 1850's.

Lockwood, Charles **Bricks & Brownstone, the New York Row House 1783-1929, an Architectural & Social History,** New York, McGraw-Hill, 1972.
Available - GPL
Although not about New England houses the helpful architectural details apply to many later houses, especially town houses.

Maass, John **The Victorian Home in America.** New York, Hawthorn Books, Inc., 1972.
 Available - GPL
  - PPL 720.973 qM11v
 This book covers Gothic Revival, Italianate, Mansard, and Queen Anne Styles.

Maine Catalog of the Historic American Buildings Survey. A list of Measured Drawings, Photographs & Written Documents in the Survey to 1974. Augusta, Maine, Maine State Museum, 1974.
 Available - GPL
  - PPL 720.9741 H673
 Compiled with an introductory essay on the historic architecture of Maine by Denys Peter Meyers. Very useful local reference materials.

Morrison, Hugh **Early American Architecture, from the First Colonial Settlement to the National Period,** N.Y. Oxford Univ. Press, 1952.
 Available - GPL
  - PPL 720.973 M87
 Comprehensive account of architecture in the American Colonies. Eight chapters related to New England.

Pierson, William H., Jr. **American Buildings and Their Architects - the Colonial and Neoclassical Styles.** Garden City, Doubleday, 1970.
 Available - GPL
  - PPL 720.973 P624

Scully, Vincent Joseph **The Shingle Style.** New Haven, Yale University Press, 1955. Revised edition - New Haven, Yale University Press, 1971.
 Available - PPL 728 qS43, 728 qS43 1971

Whiffen, Marcus **American Architecture Since 1780: A Guide to the Styles,** Boston, Mass., M.I.T. Press, 1969.
 Available - GPL
  - PPL 720.973 W57
 Brief, comprehensive, well-illustrated guide covering whole United States, 1780 to present day.

Williams, Henry Lionel and Williams, Ottalie **Guide to Old American Houses, 1700-1900. Visual History of 200 Years of American Domestic Building.** New York, A. S. Barnes, 1962.
 Available - GPL
  - PPL 728 qW723g

HOW TO RESEARCH A HOUSE

What information you might find:

When, by whom, for whom, the house was built.

What the house and property looked like.

What the owners were like.

How the owners furnished and used the house.

SOURCES OF INFORMATION

Start with:

1. Deeds. A complete title search should be performed, beginning with the present owner and working back. Check all possible spellings of names. No mention of a house does not necessarily mean that no house is present. A sudden jump in price, a division of land, or a mortgage may indicate construction of a house. An owner's profession is often given with his name. Property descriptions can be quite detailed, giving specifics about the house and surrounding land. Search a neighboring building if you become confused because an owner of the house had extensive property holdings. Registry of Deeds at CCC.

2. Maps. Look at the 1857 Cumberland County wall map; the 1871 Atlas of Cumberland County; the 1882 and following Sanborn Insurance Maps; and any other maps you can find for information about the size, shape, and materials of the house. Names of owners or occupants may be given; check them against title search. CCC, MHS, LL.

Once you have owner information from the title search, you should look at:

3. Directories. Residential and business directories are available for Portland and other communities. See when various owners lived in the house, who rented the house, what were professions of owners or occupants. MHS, LL.

4. Obituaries. Check in newspapers published immediately after a person's death. Check any obituary scrapbooks. The Maine Historical Society has scrapbooks of obituaries (and other newspaper articles) which are most helpful; check their biographical file. MHS, PPL, LL.

5. Biographies. Dictionaries of American and National Biography. Biographies collected by town, or county; college; sometimes profession. MHS, PPL, LL.

6. Family genealogies. MHS, LL.

You should investigate these primary sources:

7. Newspapers. Check old newspapers (frequently available on microfilm) from around the time the house was built for information about the building, owner, architect. MHS, PPL, LL

8. Legal documents. Wills, inventories, indentures, testimony. Registry of Probate at CCC.

9. Commercial documents. Account books, purchase orders, inventories. MHS, LL.

10. Family documents. Letters, diaries, drawings. Such items may be in the possession of a family. MHS, LL.

11. Vital statistics. Vital records of the town, census records, cemetery inscriptions, church records. Maine State Archives, Augusta. MHS, LL, TO.

Visual material is a great aid. Look for:

12. Photographs. May be in the possession of a family. MHS, LL.

13. Drawings. Sketches, architectural plans, renderings. May be in the possession of a family, of an architect. MHS, LL.

Talk to people to gather:

14. Oral evidence. Speak with former owners, neighbors, long time residents of the town. People do not always remember accurately, so oral evidence should be taken with a grain of salt. Libraries may have transcripts of previous conversations.

You should also look at these secondary sources:

15. Histories. Town or regional histories, guide books, Work Projects Administration books. MHS, LL.

16. Newspaper articles. Check indexes at libraries for articles printed in old newspapers. Check the libraries of current newspapers for more recent articles. MHS, PPL, LL.

Keep a complete list of all sources investigated, whether helpful or not, and where they are located. Include people, too.
Copy exactly. Obtain machine copies whenever possible.

LOCATION OF SOURCES

CCC Cumberland County Courthouse, 142 Federal Street, Portland, Maine.

MHS Maine Historical Society, 485 Congress Street, Portland, Maine.

PPL Portland Public Library, 619 Congress Street, Portland, Maine.

LL   Local library.

TO   Town office.

Local historical societies are frequently helpful.

The Maine State Library in Augusta has an increasing collection.

BIBLIOGRAPHY

Bullock, Orin M., Jr. **The Restoration Manual.** Norwalk, Connecticut, Silvermine Publishers Incorporated, 1966, pages 13-17.
  Available - GPL

Little, Nina Fletcher "Finding the Records of an Old House" (in **Old-Time New England,** Volume XL, No. 2, October, 1949, pages 145-148.)
  Available - GPL
         - PPL R974 S67 Art

Parker, Donald Dean **Local History How to Gather It, Write It, and Publish It.** New York, Social Science Research Council, 1944.
  Available - GPL

Rath, Frederick L., Jr., general editor **Selective Reference Guide to Historic Preservation.** Cooperstown, New York, New York State Historical Association, 1966, pages 91-115
  Available - GPL

MAKING PLANS AND KEEPING RECORDS

All findings from the following subjects should be compiled in record form by owner of restoration project. The record should include sections:

1. Existing conditions
2. Work in progress
3. History
4. Finished project

This record should be expandable (notebook) so material can be added at any time.

I PHOTOGRAPHIC RECORD

Before a shingle has been removed or a fireplace uncovered - PHOTO-GRAPH. Take pictures of the exterior from every angle and do a series of pictures of every room. Use black and white film and label each print on back.

Exterior - Photo of every side. Close-ups of cornice, doorways, one window 1st and 2nd floor and attic (any others that are different). Close-up of any outstanding features (foundation, hardware, mouldings, sidings, etc.)

Interior - Photos of each room, each wall, corner to corner, fireplaces, doors, windows, hardware, mouldings, floor, etc.

Work in progress - when the men come to work on sills and strengthen the timbers get pictures of what they uncover and their completed work.

II THE INTERIOR: HOW TO MEASURE AND DRAW IT

Measuring and Rough Drawing

The basic tools required are:

1. A 50 foot minimum measuring tape or a 6 to 10 foot tape if only a room is being measured. The tape should be subdivided into inches and not tenths of a foot (as in the case of an engineer's tape).
2. A six foot folding rule with extension on end for measuring ceiling heights.
3. A pad or clipboard with sheets of squared paper, at least 8½" x 11".

4. A medium-grade pencil - not too hard, not too soft - and a means of sharpening it.
5. An eraser.

Procedure
1. Draw sketch to scale - ¼″ = 1′0″ - measure to nearest ½″. This should be done freehand using lines of squared paper as guide.

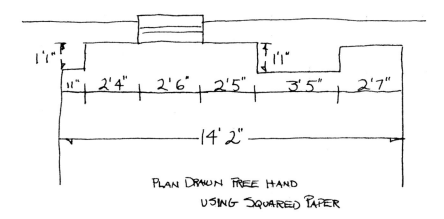

PLAN DRAWN FREE HAND
USING SQUARED PAPER

2. The sketch must show: all projections, recesses, windows, doors, and doorswings. Measuring is easier with two people. Don't expect to get all the information in one visit - even architects rarely do. Measure heights of ceilings, doors, windows.
3. All measurements should be taken to the plaster or surface and not to baseboards or projecting trim.
4. Checklist of dimensions and information required in making a measured drawing.
   A. Measure exterior, all sides.
   B. Measure interior overall and then determine wall thickness.
   C. Measure the rooms for overall sizes before going on to measure the position of the projections, alcoves, windows, and doors.
   D. Take only useful sizes and no more than necessary to locate all the major features already mentioned.
   E. Note heights (as already mentioned) of floor to ceiling, floor to floor height, the height of doors, the amount of clearance under a stairway, duct, or sloping ceiling.
   F. Carefully sketch existing stairways and, in addition to overall size and width of the runs, note the number of treads and risers from floor to floor and also whether there are winders or not.
   G. Finally, check that all elements which might be difficult or expen-

20

sive to remove, such as flues or chimney breasts, stacks and pipes, have been properly located and noted on the sketch. Structural walls should be noted and not confused with extra thick partitions used for pipe spaces.

Plan to return at least once to check some dimensions.

Basic Tools For Drawing Final Plan From Measurements
1. Pencil - H or 2H.
2. Tracing paper with lines forming ¼″ squares.
3. Straight edge clear-plastic triangle and "T" square.
4. Architect's scale ruler.

Procedure:
1. Use checklist as guide.
2. Final plan should show existing conditions. It is advisable to make a separate plan for proposed changes.

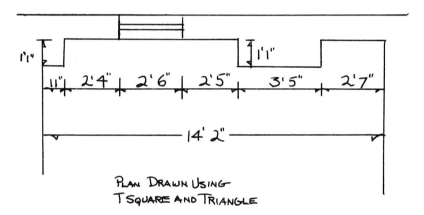

PLAN DRAWN USING
T SQUARE AND TRIANGLE

III STRUCTURAL ANALYSIS

An investigation of what is extant in the building to determine what part belongs to what era. Professional advice is usually imperative at this point and worth a great deal more than the actual cost.

Try to discover the original treatment of major features such as fireplaces, paneling, doors and windows. Try to determine which parts are oldest and which have been later additions or alterations. The examination must cover everything from foundation level to the ridge of the roof, with a watchful eye for warped corners, broken plaster, sagging floors, bulging walls, water stains around windows or on ceilings, and every other sort of evidence of structural damage.

IV DOCUMENTATION

Delve deeply into the past of the house to be rehabilitated. The research that you do will help you achieve the kind of house you want, adapted to its architectural heritage. (See: How To Research a House, in this folder)

V RESTORATION AND REHABILITATION PROGRAM

Make a careful plan, whether you intend to do the whole job at once or not. At this point it is important to consider seeking professional advice. List specifics - costs, changes in floor plans, installation of facilities and other details down to the final stage of decorating. A good plan must take into consideration the past as well as present and future needs of both house and inhabitants.

Consistency of detail in major units of architectural design is advisable (door, windows, etc.) It is not unusual to find several periods of design in one house. These changes should be preserved if the major designs are good examples of the periods they represent.

VI ACTUAL WORK - A WORD OF CAUTION, "THINK BEFORE YOU DE-STROY."

Most important - if you can find workmen who know and understand old houses, you'll have pleasanter restoration memories. No matter what your budget of time and money, do each thing well, or leave it until you can do it well.

Don't rush in where carpenters fear to tread. Wherever structural strength and practicality are involved, get professional advice.

Avoid matched boards, particularly knotty pine, if you want an antique effect. Our ancestors went to great lengths to eliminate knots from all finished boards. New work should be marked on back with date before putting in place. Use lead pencil or steel metal punches. New wood will show in black and white print if picture is taken before room is painted.

BIBLIOGRAPHY

Stephen, George **Remodeling Old Houses Without Destroying Their Character,** N.Y. Knopf 1972.
    Available - GPL
        - PPL 728 S828

McKee, Harley J. **Recording Historic Buildings.** National Park Service, 1970.
    Available - GPL

Reproducing Old Mouldings (in APT V. III no. 4, 1971, pp. 48-53.)
    Available - GPL

REPLACING ARCHITECTURAL DETAILS

A difficult problem that often occurs in restoring old buildings and houses is the necessary replacement of missing or inappropriate doors, doorways, windows, mouldings, paneling and fireplace mantels. This can involve missing parts or whole units. It is not unusual to find several periods of architectural design in one house indicating changes and remodelings that have taken place in the history of the building. SPNEA and GPL encourage preservation of these changes (even where several are evident in one room) if the major units (windows, doorways, fireplace mantels) are good examples of the periods they represent.

When considering replacement of whole units of architectural detail it is essential to do extensive research to obtain information for accurate and appropriate design. Sometimes, examples in the same building can be used. Be sure to search for discarded details (doors, mouldings, etc.) in the attic, cellar, ells, sheds and barn. Besides using available reference books, buildings of the same vintage in the surrounding area should be studied.

Some of the larger lumber companies have cabinet shops with machinery to mill mouldings. This service is best used when a large amount of a specific moulding is needed. For copying, it is necessary to provide either a small sample or a full scale profile drawn on paper. The profile can be drawn from the outline formed when a lino or profile gauge is pressed across a moulding. The gauge is obtainable at hardware stores. A lead strip can also be used to form a profile. For best results remove a strip of paint on moulding first. There are a few modern mouldings similar to the old (1880) designs which can be slightly altered on a bench saw to match the old ones. Several modern crown mouldings almost match some of the 1800 cornice mouldings and when applied where sections are missing will blend with the old. For very small missing sections (inches) a plaster cast can be made and used to mold wet plaster in place. For short lengths (up to 6') a Stanley profile plane with adjustable blades can be used. Some craftsmen have collections of old planes and can reproduce old mouldings. Further details for fabrication are on file at the GPL Resource Center and available for use to the restorer.

It is important to plan ahead when replacing any piece of architectural detail in an old building. There must be time for research and time for fabrication.

PROFILES OF TYPICAL LOCAL
19TH CENTURY MOULDINGS

BIBLIOGRAPHY

Baker, Norman B. **Early Houses of New England.** Rutland, Vermont, Tuttle, 1967.
> Available - GPL
>   - PPL 728 qB16
> *Floor plans, site plans, landscaping. Plans for reproduction houses.*

Benjamin, Asher **American Builder's Companion; or, A System of Architecture Particularly Adapted to the Present Style of Building.** Boston, R.P. & C. Williams, 1827. New York, Dover reprint, 1969.
> Available - GPL - reprint
>   - PPL - 1827 ed. Rv 720 qB46.
> *An important source for architectural detail. "Federal Neo-Classic" period. Plate 9: typical mouldings and names, measurements and geometric designs.*

Chamberlain, Narcissa **Old Rooms for New Living; Being a Collection of Early American Interiors Authentic in Design, Various in Period, and Suitable for Today's Living.** This Is a Treasury of Tradition for the Home Decorator. New York, Hastings House, 1953. 2d printing 1965.
> Available - GPL
> *Excellent for general information on periods. Interiors.*

Dietz, Albert G. **Dwelling House Construction.** Princeton, N.J., Van Nostrand 1946, revised edition Cambridge, Mass., M.I.T. Press, 1971.
> Available - GPL
>   - PPL 690 D56 1954, 1971.
> *Details of construction and modern building specifications. An invaluable handbook on methods and materials.*

Downing, Andrew Jackson **Architecture of Country Houses, including Designs for Cottages and Farm-houses, and Villas, with Remarks on Interiors, Furniture, and the Best Modes of Warming and Ventilation.** New York, Appleton, 1850. New York, Dover reprint, 1969.
> Available - GPL
> *Good source for general information on country Victorian and Gothic Revival.*

Duprey, Kenneth **Old Houses on Nantucket.** New York, Architectural Book Pub. Co., 1959.
> Available - GPL
>   - PPL 728 qD94
> *Interiors, good photographs, local.*

Hamlin, Talbot **Greek Revival Architecture in America; Being an Account of Important Trends in American Architecture and American Life Prior to the War Between the States.** New York, Oxford Univ. Press, 1944. New York, Dover reprint, 1964.
> Available - GPL
>   - PPL 724 H22
> *Excellent for obtaining general information. Mostly exteriors. Excellent bibliography and list of Greek Revival architects and their writings.*

Howells, John Mead **Architectural Heritage of the Piscataqua; Houses and Gardens of the Portsmouth District of Maine and New Hampshire.** New York, Architectural Book Pub., Inc., 1937, 1965.
> Available - GPL 1965 reprint.
>   - PPL 1937 ed. R728 qH85.
> *Important source for New England detail. Photos and elevations, profiles, plans.*

Howells, John Mead **Lost Examples of Colonial Architecture; Buildings That Have Disappeared or Been So Altered as to be Denatured; Public Buildings, Semi-Public, Churches, Cottages, Country Houses, Town Houses, Interiors, Details.** New York, W. Helburn, 1931. New York, Dover reprint, 1963.
> Available - GPL
>   - PPL 1931 ed. R724.9 qH85.
> *Very good photos of details. Interior and exterior.*

Kelly, J. Frederick **Early Domestic Architecture of Connecticut.** New Haven, Yale Univ. Press, 1924. New York, Dover reprint, 1963.
> Available - GPL Dover reprint.
>   - PPL 1924 ed. R728 qK29
> *Important source for early details.*
> *Chapter   V-Exterior Overhang.*
> *Chapter   IX-Windows.*
> *Chapter   X & XI-Entrances - Early & Later.*
> *Chapter   XII-Main Cornice.*
> *Chapter XII-XIV-Excellent general and specific information on interiors.*

Kettell, Russell Hawes, **Early American Rooms: a Consideration of the Changes in Style Between the Arrival of the Mayflower and the Civil War in the Regions Originally Settled by the English and the Dutch, 1650-1858.** Portland, Maine, Southworth Press, 1936. New York, Dover reprint, 1967.
> Available - GPL Dover reprint.
>   - PPL 1936 ed. R747 qK43 Southworth.
> *An important source for architectural detail. Interiors. Excellent elevations, sections and profiles. Also period furnishings.*

Kimball, Sidney Fiske **Domestic Architecture of the American Colonies and of the Early Republic.**
New York, Scribner's, 1922. New York, Dover reprint, 1966.
Available - GPL Dover reprint.
- PPL 1922 ed. R728 qK49.
Very general - some excellent photos of the Federal Period. Interiors, mantels, cupboards.

LaFever, Minard **Modern Builder's Guide.** Henry C. Sleight - Collins and Hannay, 1833. New
York, Dover reprint, 1969.
Available - GPL - Dover reprint.
*Greek Revival. Beautiful line drawings of motifs and details of doorways, mouldings, cornice,
mantels, stairs. Glossary of technical terms. Geometric forms. Plaster and plaster moulding,
page 124.*

Pierson, William H., Jr. **American Buildings and Their Architects - the Colonial and Neoclassical
Styles.** Garden City, Doubleday, 1970.
Available - GPL - Dover reprint.
- PPL 720.973 P624.
*An architectural analysis and evaluation of Early American buildings and how American archi-
tects adapted the building traditions of Europe.*

Sloane, Eric **Reverence for Wood.** New York, W. Funk, 1965.
Available - PPL 620.12 qS63.
*Excellent for basic information about early construction, pages 30-33. Early doors, pages 79 &
80, wainscoting, sheathing, panels.*

Stephen, George **Remodeling Old Houses Without Destroying Their Character.** New York, Knopf,
1972.
Available - GPL
- PPL 728 S828.
*Town houses - good examples of use of new materials. Proportions. How to measure and draw
plans.*

Williams, Henry Lionel and Williams, Ottalie **Old American Houses 1700-1850. How to Restore,
Remodel and Reproduce Them.** New York, Bonanza, 1957.
Available - GPL
*Good "how to" information for restorer to read before attempting restoration. Pages 90-99
mouldings, Page 99 paneling.*

APT—Bulletin - Vol. III No. 4, 1971, Pages 48-53. Lee H. Nelson, Architect. Nat. Park Ser., Phil.,
Pa.
Available - GPL
Simplified methods for producing wood mouldings.

FIREPLACES AND CHIMNEYS

Until the middle of the nineteenth century, fireplaces and their chimneys governed the way a house was built, and a set floor plan resulted.

In the early days the great kitchen fireplace provided heat, cooking, and lighting, and most of the living in a small house was done around it. Larger houses would have other fireplaces for use at different times. Many bedrooms off, or over, the kitchen were not provided with their own fireplaces, supposedly getting sufficient heat from the one constantly burning fire; a grating in the kitchen ceiling still often survives today. A hole to permit warm air to rise through the ceiling is found in the eighteenth century Parson Smith House, Windham. A cast-iron grating would date from the stove era, where it served the same purpose.

Large fireplaces are attractive to look at but are not very efficient. The cavernous early fireplace, complete with oven in its rear wall and heavy wooden lintel, in a room with exposed timber framing and beams, is very appealing, but belongs strictly to the Early American period before about 1730. While this is an attractive style to copy and widely admired today it should in no way be regarded as an authentic way of "restoring" a house in this area, where we have no houses built before the Colonial (or Georgian) period. Even the earliest permanent houses in this area would usually have had plastered ceilings, with the chimney wall paneled or plastered and all the framing timbers neatly cased.

A satisfactory compromise can often be achieved by using the much admired handhewn beams and large fireplace in an ell kitchen or family room. Ells tend to have been altered to suit the needs and tastes of succeeding generations of owners, and this can be done very successfully without destroying the integrity (and hence the resale value) of the main house. This is particularly important where good original features (of whatever period) still exist - such as ceilings, woodwork and fireplaces.

CHANGING STYLES OF FIREPLACES. Fireplaces change as fashion and living styles change. They tend to get progressively smaller and shallower. Sometimes one may find as many as three different fireplaces built within each other before they were covered over completely to install a stove. There may have been a stove there for well over a hundred years. Stoves still function efficiently today and in many cases it may be practical to leave the stove in place, or to replace it if only the stovepipe hole remains.

Think carefully before opening up a fireplace. The one you reveal so proudly may present you with some problems: it may not ever have been very efficient, and it is almost certain to need some professional attention before it is safe to use.

Throughout the period when houses were heated by fires the fireplace was the focal point of the room. Even when it was not in use during the summer it was often emphasized by an attractive cover, the decorated "Fireboard". In keeping with the architectural style of the room the fireboards were embellished with graining, stenciling, freehand paintings of flowers, vases, urns, fans or **trompe l'oeil**. Special wallpaper panels could also be bought for the purpose (see wallpaper section).

In the Victorian period elaborate cast-iron grills were often found, or some decorative filling for the complex small cast-iron coal grates.

Fireboards are still a practical and attractive solution today where a fireplace cannot be opened up; or whenever a fireplace is not in use it discourages draughts... and cats! They are not hard to recreate in a number of different ways mentioned above.

CHIMNEYS need careful inspection, flues often need lining, dampers have to be installed. A possible temporary solution is to install a removable piece of thick foil-backed insulation material, cut to size, which will wedge in the chimney when the fireplace is not in use. A shaped piece of metal, slotted or wedged in, will also serve in place of a damper. Chimney stacks may need to be rebuilt from the attic up; rain running down the chimney causes the soft old brick to crumble and flake off, and the mortar to loosen and fall out. Even if the brick is new, repointing the brickwork and reflashing the chimney where it comes through the roof are likely to be necessary.

In many cases the chimney stack has been rebuilt during the stove era and a spindly vestige is all that remains above the roof. Rebuilding this to its original dimensions, while expensive, will greatly enhance the appearance of the whole house.

MASONS. Good masons who enjoy working with old houses are scarce, slow to come, and expensive. It is a highly skilled and very traditional trade, but old methods and the finish appropriate to old houses are not necessarily understood by all masons. Therefore, it will really pay you to research the subject, and to study houses of a similar period, preferably those in the same locality. Often details missing in yours have survived elsewhere. Try to see other work done by the mason you select. Brick is an expensive and very permanent material and you will have to look at it for a long time. Such details as the brick size, color and texture, the proportion of brick to the width of the mortar joints, and the color of the mortar itself are all vital to the pleasing effect of the finished work. (See material available at the GPL Resource Center).

FIREPLACE FINISH. Much old brickwork that is revealed during renovation is rather rough and clumsy, clearly never intended to be left exposed to the eye. Masons always took pride in their work and never left a finished surface looking like this even in the early days. The bricks may have been uneven in size (they were made by hand) but they were neatly and carefully set with comparatively narrow mortar lines. The surround to the fireplace in Georgian and Federal parlors and bedrooms was usually finished with marble, slate, or other stone, tile, or brick covered with cement. Where the brick facing is now exposed there is usually clear indication on the adjoining woodwork that the brick originally had a covering of plaster or cement on it, and this should be replaced if the original effect is to be achieved. A carefully designed painted wooden mantelpiece in keeping with the woodwork in the rest of the room was much emphasized during the Georgian and Federal periods and some lovely ingenious examples still exist; many of these were copied from plates in the "Architects and Builders" handbooks, which were now readily available.

During the Greek Revival period, the taste for plain smooth surfaces became dominant and the much smaller fire chamber may have a wide, smoothly cemented surround. The mantelpiece even in the most formal houses was of far less importance, many being plain to the point of clumsiness in a room with otherwise quite elaborate mouldings and woodwork.

By the 1840's-70's stoves became increasingly popular, but coal grates in marble, slate or soapstone-faced fireplaces are often found, and, together with Franklin stoves and iron "Fire Frames", were readily available both locally and through trade catalogues. The Victorian Period also saw a great elaboration of woodwork, mostly machine made. Some very ornate mantelpieces in heavy, dark wood, sometimes incorporating mirrors or ceramic tiles, were popular and could be supplied complete by local lumber mills. The open fire had practically disappeared and the stove became the universal source of heat until the advent of the furnace.

KITCHEN FIREPLACES. In the kitchen the big open cooking fire of the Early American Period became smaller during the Georgian and Federal Periods thus increasing its efficiency. It acquired a swing-out crane for suspending its cooking pots which, together with ovens beside the fireplace instead of inconveniently in the rear wall, greatly facilitated the cooking. The heavy wooden lintel which supported the brickwork over the Early American fireplace gave way to one made of thin wrought iron which did not show (it was covered by cement). Quarried granite lintels were also used in some districts. A narrow mantel shelf, supported by simple brackets or a bed mold, is often found during the Georgian and Federal period with a paneled, and later plastered, fireplace wall. (NOTE: Very few houses that we know of locally have an original wooden lintel; these lintels belong to an earlier era than most existing houses in Maine).

The oven mouths were covered with wooden paneled or batten doors when

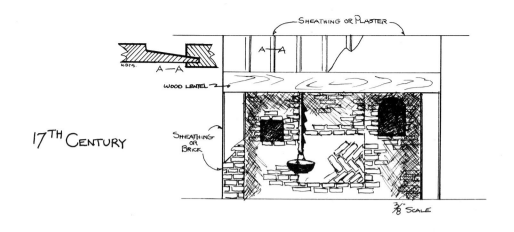

SHEATHING OR PLASTER

A — A

WOOD LENTEL

SHEATHING OR BRICK

17ᵀᴴ CENTURY

⅞" SCALE

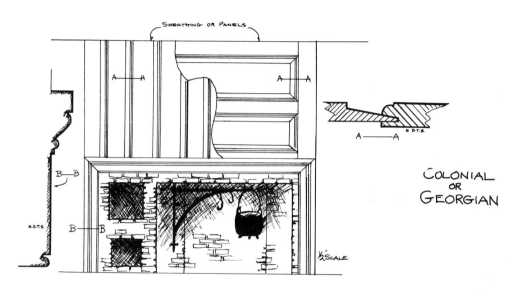

SHEATHING OR PANELS

A — A

A — A

B — B

N.D.T.S.

B — B

N.D.T.S.

COLONIAL OR GEORGIAN

½" SCALE

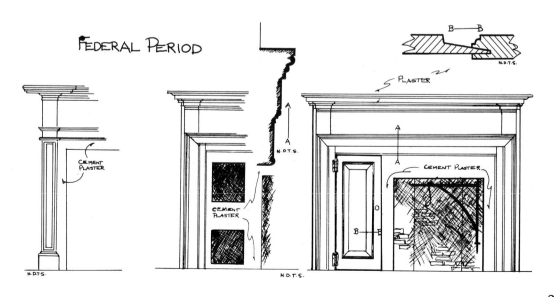

FEDERAL PERIOD

CEMENT PLASTER

CEMENT PLASTER

CEMENT PLASTER

N.D.T.S.

N.D.T.S.

B — B

N.D.T.S.

PLASTER

A

A

CEMENT PLASTER

B — B

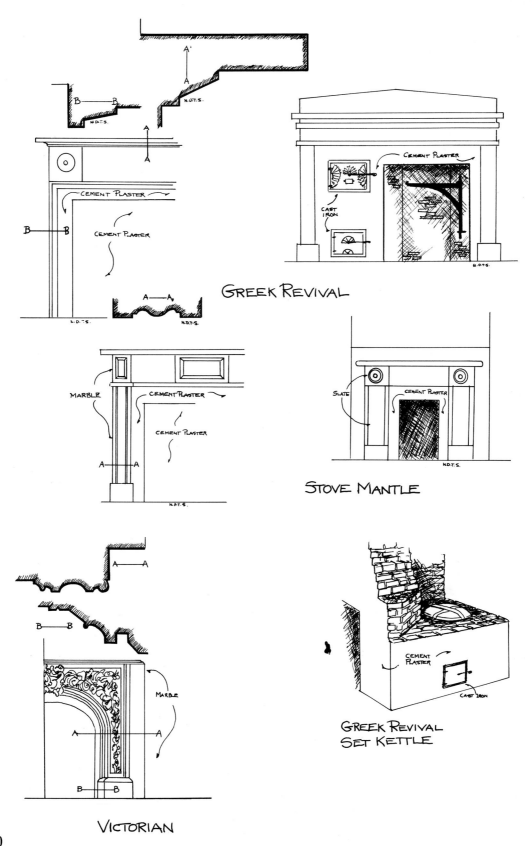

GREEK REVIVAL

STOVE MANTLE

GREEK REVIVAL
SET KETTLE

VICTORIAN

30

not in use, or later (early 1820's) were equipped with cast-iron oven doors, attractively decorated with fan designs. The entire brick face surrounding these doors was cemented over to produce a smooth, neat appearance, in keeping with the plain surfaces favored by the Greek Revival style. A plain heavy mantel shelf, supported by brackets, pilasters or a simple bed mold, usually spanned the whole cooking fireplace.

All fireplace openings had diminished in size by this period, becoming much shallower and narrower in proportion to their height, often almost square.

COOKING STOVES. During the 1840's-60's the cooking and heating stove began to take over. In many instances it was installed in front of a now blocked kitchen fireplace while retaining the brick ovens beside it. Examples of this will often be found in the ell where it formed part of the "summer kitchen" where many of the heavy household chores were performed. Often a large iron "Set Kettle" is found behind or to one side of the old fireplace, with its own separate fire chamber beneath to heat a large supply of hot water for laundry, etc. This may by today have been removed, but the remains of it are sometimes visible in an adjacent closet or entry way. This arrangement also continued on into the stove era of the Victorian period; a very simple mantel shelf is usually found here, sometimes now supported by cast iron brackets.

CENTRAL HEATING came first to the large public buildings of the metropolitan areas towards the end of the eighteenth century. It was not a feature of private houses in this area until the late nineteenth century. Not until central heating and insulation became really efficient and reliable could New Englanders afford the luxury of opening up their fireplaces again. Some of the early elaborate cast-iron radiators are interesting period pieces and should be retained where possible.

Sometimes an eager search for an old fireplace in a newly acquired house leads to the disappointing discovery that the chimney itself has been removed or was designed to serve only a stove. The furnace flue may have been taken up through a blocked fireplace; and it may be possible to rectify this by building an additional flue alongside the existing chimney if there is adjoining closet space. Sometimes, however, beneath an unlikely looking wall with modern finish (and even with baseboard heating) you may discover a fine old fireplace waiting to be uncovered, complete even to the paneling over the mantel, entirely hidden by plaster and wallpaper. Careful measuring and a little discreet prodding and tapping, following clues of cracked plaster and unaccounted for spaces, can reveal some pleasant surprises. But, one word of advice. Do it before you decide to install your washing machine on that wall.

BIBLIOGRAPHY

Congdon, H. W. **Early American Homes for Today; a Treasury of Decorative Details and Restoration Procedures.** Rutland, Vermont, Tuttle, 1963. Second printing 1969.

Available - GPL
- PPL 728 qC74e
Chapter VIII Chimneys, Fireplaces.
Chapter IX Mantels.
Good photos of Federal mantels.

Dietz, Albert G. **Dwelling House Construction**, Princeton, N.J. VanNostrand, 1946. Revised edition Cambridge, Mass. M.I.T. Press, 1971. Chimneys - Fireplaces, Chapter 6, pp. 126-142. Modern specifications - Construction information.
Available - GPL

Downing, Andrew Jackson **Architecture of Country Houses, including Designs for Cottages and Farm-houses, and Villas, with Remarks on Interiors, Furniture, and the Best Modes of Warming and Ventilating** New York, Appleton, 1850. New York, Dover reprint, 1969.
Available - GPL
- PPL 749 F852
Section VII pp. 174-180 Chimneys, Fireplaces.
Section XIII pp. 461-484 Warming Ventilating.

Eberlein, H. D. and Hubbard, C. V. D. **Colonial Interiors: Federal and Greek Revival.** Third series. New York, W. Helburn, 1938.
Available - PPL R728 qE16c
No text. Photographs & architectural drawings of fireplace walls and mantels. Pl. 53-145.

French, Leigh, Jr. **Colonial Interiors, First Series; Photographs and Measured Drawings of the Colonial and Early Federal Periods.** New York, W. Helburn, 1923. Reprinted, Bonanza, N.Y. (no date.)
Available - PPL R728 qF87
Mostly southern New England. No text. Photographs (Pl 1-56) & architectural drawings (PL 107-124) of fireplace walls and mantels.

Gould, Mary Earle **Early American House.** Rutland, Vermont, Tuttle 1949, Revised Edition, 1965.
Good chapters on chimneys and fireplaces, pp. 44-66. Helpful photographs.

Kauffman, Henry J. **American Fireplace; Chimneys, Mantelpieces, Fireplaces and Accessories.** Nashville, T. Nelson, 1972.
Available - GPL
- PPL 749 qK21am
Recently published comprehensive book on the subject, arranged chronologically.

McKee, Harley J. **Introduction to Early American Masonry: Stone, Brick, Mortar & Plaster.** Washington, D.C., National Trust, Columbia University 1973.
Available - GPL

Orton, Vrest **Observations on the Forgotten Art of Building a Good Fireplace.** Dublin, N.H. Yankee, 1969.
Available - GPL
- PPL 728.6 078
Part IV, pp. 40-60 has some useful diagrams and measurements.

Williams, Henry Lionel and Williams, Ottalie **Old American Houses 1700-1850. How to Restore, Remodel and Reproduce Them.** New York, Bonanza, 1957.
Available - GPL
Useful for general information and restoration procedures.

STOVES

Curtis, Will & Jane **Antique Woodstoves: Artistry in Iron.** Kennebunk, Me., Star Press 1974.
Photographic survey with descriptive text.

Mercer, Henry C. **Bible in Iron.** Doylestown, Pa., Bucks County Historical Society, Third edition, 1961.
Available - GPL
Pre-Revolutionary stove manufacture. Mainly Pennsylvania.

Pierce, Josephine H. **Fire on the Hearth.** Springfield, Mass., 1951.
Evolution of the heating stove. Especially late 19th century.

PERIODICALS

A P T Bulletin. V. 3, Nos. 2-3, 1971. **Issue on Stoves.** Also possible subsequent articles.
Available - GPL

Old House Journal
Available - GPL
Continues to have relevant articles on fireplaces and stoves.

Old Time New England
Available - GPL
- PPL R974 S67 Art
Has had various articles on stoves. Valuable because our most local reference source.

LIGHTING

What were the lighting devices of the early New Englanders? Probably messy, smelly grease lamps. Any grease that would burn, kitchen fats or fish oil, would have been used for illumination up through the 18th century, and well into the 19th in country areas. The device now called a Betty lamp, an improvement upon the primitive cruse which was a grease filled dish with a lip in which the wick rested, was widely used. This lamp of iron in a boat shape that had changed little since the days of ancient Rome, burned a piece of twisted fiber floating in oil or grease set in a trough, a little back of the lip. Hinged covers limited the size of the flame.

Another source of illumination was the rush light, the pith of the common reed or cattail dipped in tallow and fastened in a scissorslike holder. This feeble light, or the smouldering knot of a pitch pine limb resting on the hearth or secured in a viselike arrangement, was often the only light other than that of the open fire in a 17th Century kitchen.

It would be difficult to adapt such lighting to modern living, but then houses, like people, develop with age, and as the interior of the house has changed, the ways of lighting it have also altered. There is probably in each building at least one period that predominates, and if that period is well represented and worthy of being emphasized, the lighting devices of its time could be those chosen for use. In the case of a diversity of periods apparent throughout the house, a variety of lighting devices could be used in keeping with the architecture of the individual room.

The 18th Century offers a wide variety of lighting types to choose from. The crude early lamps gradually became replaced by those having a base surmounted by a closed font for fuel, and one or more vertical tubes through which the wick (or wicks) was pulled. The improved types were of tin, pewter, Britannia ware, brass, glass or silver depending upon the prosperity of the owner. These lamps burned fish or whale oil, spermaceti from the head of the cachelot whale being the most efficient. Later lard or lard oil was used, sometimes with alcohol. Adding a small amount of camphor improved the odor. This mixture was not the fuel called camphene, however, which was introduced in the mid-19th Century. Camphene contained both turpentine and alcohol, and though producing a fine clear light was highly explosive and its use was soon discontinued.

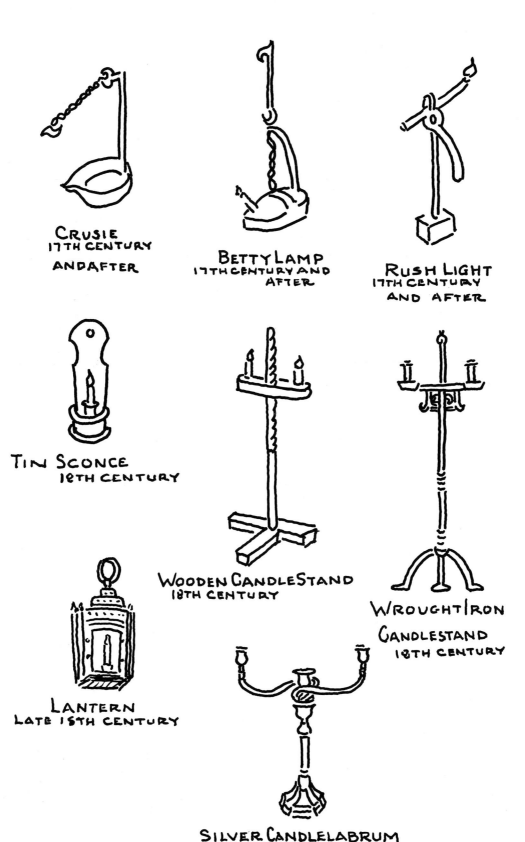

CRUSIE
17TH CENTURY
AND AFTER

BETTY LAMP
17TH CENTURY AND
AFTER

RUSH LIGHT
17TH CENTURY
AND AFTER

TIN SCONCE
18TH CENTURY

WOODEN CANDLE STAND
18TH CENTURY

WROUGHT IRON
CANDLESTAND
18TH CENTURY

LANTERN
LATE 18TH CENTURY

SILVER CANDLELABRUM
LATE 18TH CENTURY

CONVEX GIRONDOLE MIRROR WITH CANDLES
EARLY 19TH CENTURY

PEWTER WHALE OIL LAMP
1820 AND AFTER

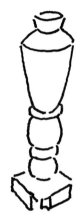

GLASS WHALE OIL LAMP
1ST HALF 19TH CENTURY

ARGAND LAMP
1820-50

KEROSENE LAMP
1860S AND AFTER

ASTRAL LAMP
1820S THROUGH 70S

KEROSENE LAMP
1860S AND AFTER

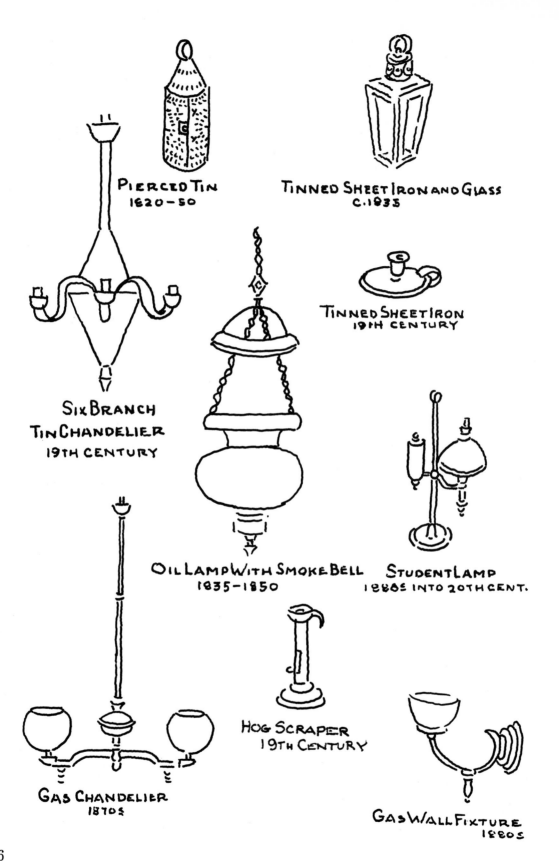

PIERCED TIN
1820-50

TINNED SHEET IRON AND GLASS
C.1835

TINNED SHEET IRON
19TH CENTURY

SIX BRANCH
TIN CHANDELIER
19TH CENTURY

OIL LAMP WITH SMOKE BELL
1835-1850

STUDENT LAMP
1880S INTO 20TH CENT.

HOG SCRAPER
19TH CENTURY

GAS CHANDELIER
1870S

GAS WALL FIXTURE
1880S

In 1783 a Swiss by the name of Aimé Argand perfected a new type of lamp burner using a cylindrical wick mounted between two metal tubes. The wick extended through and below the oil reservoir of the lamp. Holes at the bottom of the burner admitted air, creating a draft within as well as without the wick. The oil was fed to the burner from a raised reservoir which facilitated the flow of fuel. A tall cylindrical chimney further improved the draft. Though these lamps were popular and burned most efficiently, the raised reservoir cast a shadow on the lighted area lessening the practicality of the device.

An improvement upon this invention was the so-called Astral lamp, though it was manufactured under many other names. Here the reservoir was in the form of a narrow ring placed at the level of the burner. The oil was fed through a slender tube. The lamp was tall and the light issued from above the burner.

The Solar lamp was a follower of the Astral. Developed in the mid-19th Century it had a deflector shaped like an inverted saucer with the draft issuing against the flame of an Argand burner. Since the heat was directed toward the reservoir this lamp could use a heavier fluid such as lard which gave an intense white light.

In 1854 kerosene, distilled from coal and petroleum, was introduced and became the generally used lamp fuel. This oil was more efficient, safer and less expensive than those which had preceded it. Lamps using kerosene were produced in many different forms and varieties of materials.

Though kerosene lighting was the illumination most widely used in America in the latter half of the 19th Century, lighting by gas had been used in England since 1798 and the city of London was provided with gas in 1812. In 1816 a theater was illuminated in Philadelphia, and by 1836 that city as well as Baltimore, New York, and Boston could supply gas to their residents. Gas was introduced in Portland, Maine, in 1849, and the city streets illuminated with 297 gas lamps in 1864.

Many of the oil fed lighting devices were converted to gas, and many new and elaborate forms were developed. Gas could, however, be used only by the city dweller, where it was available to the consumer affluent enough to subscribe to its use. Upon the advent of electricity, it was only where power lines were installed that inhabitants could have the advantage of electric lighting. Until well into the 20th Century, therefore, much of rural America was still being lighted by kerosene lamps.

Examples of gas lighting devices may be seen in Portland in the Neal Dow House and in the Victoria Mansion. Neal Dow was president of the Portland Gas Company.

With the more expensive earlier fuels only the well-to-do could afford to use a hanging lamp which required the fueling of a large reservoir. With the introduction of kerosene, hanging lamps in cheaper materials and in greater number appeared upon the market within the price range of the less affluent citizen.

Some of these hanging lights were modeled upon the chandelier, which was, of course, a candle holder suspended from the ceiling. The arms of the chandelier extending at right angles from a central shaft held sockets for the reception of candles. In the hanging oil light, the arms had become pipes feeding several lights surrounding a reservoir in the center. This new type of chandelier was generally supported by chains. One can see how such a device could be converted to the use of gas by using the pipes for conducting the illuminant to the burners.

In another type of hanging light the fuel was contained in a font below the burner, which was surrounded by a glass globe or urn open at the top and hung by chains from the ceiling. A smoke bell was usually suspended above the opening to protect the paint or wall paper. This type of light is often reproduced as an electric fixture, and in the proper setting makes an efficient light for an entrance hall.

In the above resumé we have mentioned only briefly the subject of candles which, of course, had been known at least since Roman times. They were a more expensive source of light than the humble greases of the kitchen. In New England they were used less generally than oil, except by the well-to-do citizens.

The best candles were of beeswax, but this was often adulterated with resin, suet, white lead, potato starch, or for those of more enduring quality, with spermaceti. Very fine candles were made entirely of spermaceti oil. Stearine was developed in 1823 but not perfected until the end of the century. Candles of this substance burn with a clear smokeless flame and don't bend when warmed. Paraffin wax derived from petroleum produced candles with an even more brilliant flame than stearine, but without the non-bending quality of the wax. Through experimentation a mixture of stearine and paraffin was arrived at, which produced the best quality of the candles we use today.

Candles in the 17th, 18th and first of the 19th Century were generally made at home by the housewife, though itinerant wax chandlers often assisted in the process or supervised it. Vegetable oils such as candleberry, myrtle, or bayberry sometimes replaced or supplemented the customary animal fats, but beef suet or mutton tallow were most widely employed until the introduction of petroleum.

Candles were made either by dipping the wick into the fat or wax, or by pouring the molten material into a metal mold into which the wick had been suspended. Many types of candle holder were used; single candlesticks; candelabra with multiple arms; lanterns with the candle inside a framework of wood or metal with the openings protected by horn, glass or sometimes mica; candlestands where the receptacle for one or more candles was raised to waist height or higher by a shaft issuing from a support on the floor; and sconces, candle brackets affixed to the wall or to a piece of furniture. Pierced tin lanterns, such as the type erroneously called "Paul Revere", were for outdoors and barn use as were the other lanterns.

Not until after 1879, the year that Thomas Edison invented the incandescent lamp, could electric lighting begin to be considered for general illumination. In 1882 the first commercial power station was opened in New York City and in 1883 electricity was first used for illumination in Portland, Maine. Much as we may tell ourselves that as owners of old houses we are dwelling in the light of the past, all but the most dedicated among us are truly basking in the illumination of the incandescent Thomas. Users of old lighting devices convert them to electricity and purchasers of reproductions buy those already wired for use.

We now approach the problem of mechanized living within the framework of a hand-crafted background.

A house that has never had electricity installed presents fewer problems for the restorer than one that has been electrified before the days of modern conveniences, or has had amateurish or haphazard installations of facilities.

The safest and most sightly method of installing power is through an underground conduit. If the walls are hollow the wiring can be carried in them to outlets by cable. If the walls are solid, arrangements must be made to hide the wiring, either in closets, through an enlargement of the covering of corner posts, or, if necessary, by unobtrusively extending the wires along the top of the baseboard and painting them to match.

Outlets should be placed as inconspicuously as possible in the plaster, not the woodwork.

There are available many good reproductions of lamps and lanterns of the various periods in American lighting. There are also many poor imitations of lighting devices on the market. Study your period before investing. A sense of good line, proportion and suitability will of course guide the discerning buyer.

Old oil lamps and even candlesticks can be electrified by a competent dealer or on a do-it-yourself basis by using the adapters sold in hardware stores or by catalog.

Many chandeliers are on the market, some with electrified candles, some with a hidden light directed downward from a central cone surrounded by sockets for wax candles.

Beware of the selection of devices too early or too late for the period of the house or your furnishings. Such choices can be as great an eyesore in a well planned room as the most blatantly garish of modern fixtures. Though temptingly appealing in naiveté of form and execution, an early iron chandelier hung from a smoothly plastered ceiling becomes an anomaly in a Federal dining room.

Indirect lighting can be used most effectively. The source of light is often hidden behind a fascia board, as over a sink, or in a window embrasure. It can be installed inside a cupboard to illuminate a collection, behind a cornice, or even from the floor directed upward if well disguised by a stationary object that suits the area.

Exterior lighting of doorways, patios and porticos is often a problem. Side lights at an entrance can disfigure a beautifully proportioned design. Here also indirect lighting can be employed. It may be directed from a tree, another building, or, if there is a power company pole near enough, an area light can be installed there by the company and paid for on the monthly bill.

Convenience, quality and source of light are all very important factors in restoring a house for modern living. Placing of furniture and planning for the locations of work, eating, recreation, reading and appliances must be done before an electrician is engaged. Careful pre-planning can obviate late disruption to rectify mistakes.

We are not content to live with the inconveniences of our ancestors, but we can preserve and emphasize the grace and dignity of our old houses adapted to modern living. The source and type of light contributes substantially to an atmosphere which, though it does not recreate the past, does establish a continuity with the lives of preceding generations of residents.

SOURCES

See catalogs in GPL Resource Center

Angelo Bros.
  Philadelphia, Pa. (wholesale)
  Lamp parts - available at:
  House of Lights, 510 Cumberland Ave., Portland, Me. 04101

Authentic Designs
  139 E. 61st St., New York 10021
  Handcrafted re-creations and adaptations of early American lighting fixtures.

Ball and Ball
  "Whitford" 463 W. Lincoln Highway, Exton, Pa. 19341.
  Reproductions of 18th Century lighting fixtures.

Lester H. Berry
  1108 Pine St., Philadelphia, Pa. 19107.
  Reproduction lighting fixtures of museum quality.

Brickmans, Inc.
  4-6 Lowell St., Boston, Mass. 02114.

Cohasset Colonials
  Cohasset, Mass. 02025.
  Reproductions of early American lighting fixtures.

deSherbinin, W. N.
  Hawleyville, Conn. 06440.
  Lamp adapters, replacement glass, lamp parts, lamp kits (wholesale only).

Diamond Lamp Studio
  212 E. 54th St., New York 10022.
  Provides shades for antique lamps, makes, mounts and repairs lamps.

The Essex Forge
  Old Dennison Rd., Essex, Conn. 06426
  Makes copies of old chandeliers, sconces, lanterns, etc.

Gem Monogram and Cut Glass Corp.
  623 Broadway, New York 10012.
  Repairs glass lamps and shades; makes custom chandeliers in glass.

Grand Brass and Electrical Supply Co.
  221 Grand St., New York 10013.
  Stocks some 25,000 items for replacing or repairing lamps.

Heritage Lanterns
  Sea Meadows Lane, Cousins Island, Yarmouth, Me. 04096.
  Reproductions of early American lighting fixtures.

King's Chandelier Co.
  Dept. B-117, Eden (Leaksville) N.C. 27288.

George Kovacs
  831 Madison Ave., New York 10021.
  Modern and indirect lighting of high quality.

The Lampcrafters
Box 501, Lawrenceville, Ga. 30245.
Handmade antique lighting reproductions.

The Lennox Shop
1127 Broadway, Hewlett, N.Y. 11557.
Handmade reproductions of lighting devices.

The Lighthouse, Will Bartlett
The Board-Eddy Rd., Dover Foxcroft, Me. 04426.
Antique and reproductions of American lighting devices.

Louis Maltia
980 Second Ave., New York 10022.
Electrifies lamps, chandeliers, sconces; matches or duplicates missing parts. One of a kind - no catalogue.

Oaklawn Metal Craft
Dallas and David John
Route 202, Lahaska, Pa. 18931
Specializes in lighting fixtures.

The Old Country Store
West Mansfield Village, Mass. 02083.
Reproductions of lighting devices.

Old Guilford Forge
Guilford, Conn. 06437

Period Furniture Hardware Co., Inc.
123 Charles St., Boston, Mass. 02114.
Authentic reproductions of period lighting fixtures.

Rosetta Lighting Studios
21 W. 46th St., New York 10036.

The Ruby Lighting Corporation
128 Fifth Ave., New York 10011.
Reproductions of lighting devices including the Victorian period.

D. C. Ryan - The Yellow Gambrel
1700 Old Post Road, Old Saybrook, Conn. 06415.
Reproductions of 17th and 18th century American lighting devices.

William Spencer
1041-47 North Pease St., Bridgeton, N.J. 08302.
Reproductions of lighting devices and of glass parts for lamps.

The Stiffel Company
Chicago, Ill. 60610.
Reproductions and adaptations of antique lighting devices.

Studio Eight Lighting
1860 Smithtown Ave., Ronkonkoma, N.Y. 11779.
Well designed modern and indirect lighting devices.

Village Forge and Tin Shop
598 Union St., No. Marshfield, Mass. 02059.
Handmade reproductions of early American lighting devices.

Williamsburg Reproductions
Craft House, Williamsburg, Virginia 23181.
Reproductions of early American lighting devices.

Wilson's Country House
P.O Box 244, 33 Saddle Ridge Drive, Simsbury, Conn. 06070
Reproductions of early American lighting devices.

BIBLIOGRAPHY

Antiques **Collectors and Collections; the Antiques Anniversary Book.** Edited by Alice Winchester and the Staff of Antiques Magazine. New York, 1961, pp. 39-48. Darbee, Herbert C. **Light America Lived By.**
Available - PPL 749 qA63c
Excellent photographs and description of lighting devices from the Wells Collection, Old Sturbridge Village.

Butler, Joseph T. **Candleholders in America 1650-1900.** New York, Bonanza, 1967.
Available - PPL 749 qB98c
A comprehensive collection of American and European candle fixtures used in America. Excellent photographs and reproductions of paintings or drawings from various periods showing lighting devices of the time in use.

Christensen, Erwin O. **Index of American Design.** New York, Macmillan, 1950.
Available - PPL R709.73 qC55i also circulating copy.
Very few but good illustrations of lighting devices.

Darbee, Herbert C. **Glossary of Old Lamps**
American Association for State and Local History No. 30.
History News
Available - GPL

Drepperd, Carl W. **Victorian, the Cinderella of Antiques.** Garden City, N.Y. Doubleday, 1950.
Available - PPL 749 D77v
Examples of esthetically appalling Victorian lamps.

Freeman, Larry **Lights on Old Lamps.** Watkins Glen, New York, Century House, 1944. Rev. ed., 1955.
Available - PPL 749 F85L 1955 ed.
Many illustrations, particularly reproductions of advertisements of 19th Century lamps. Interesting for illustrations showing lamps parts, means of operation, and for pictures of Victorian chandeliers.

Hayward, Arthur H. **Colonial Lighting.** Boston, B. J. Brimmer, 1923.   3d enlarged ed., New York, Dover, 1962.
Available - GPL 1962 ed.
         - PPL 1923 ed. R749 H42
Many photographs of lighting devices from ancient times through 1880's. Though the Colonial period is represented the title is descriptive of only a portion of the book. If approximate dates of fixtures shown had been given the photographs would be more helpful.

Hebard, Helen Brigham **Early Lighting in New England 1620-1861.** Rutland, Vermont, Tuttle, 1964.
Available - PPL 749 H44
History of lighting in America from early settlements through 19th Century.   Some good photographs.

Keyes, Willard Emerson **Miniature glass lamps.**   (in Antiques, v. 32, no. 3, Sept. 1937, pp. 125-127)
Available - PPL R050 A63 Art

Lichten, Frances **Decorative Art of Victoria's Era.**   New York, Scribner, 1950.
Available - PPL R747 qL69
Few photographs of lamps and chandeliers in period settings.

Life (Chicago) **America's Arts and Skills.** Dutton, 1957.
Available - PPL 709.73 fL72
Incidental pictures of lighting devices in photographs of rooms.

MacSwiggan, A. E. **Fairy Lamps; Evening's Glow of Yesteryear.** New York, Fountainhead, 1962.
Available - PPL 749 M17
Good illustrations and reproductions of advertisements of 19th Century Fairy lamps.

New York. Metropolitan Museum of Art **19th Century America. Furniture and Other Decorative Arts, 100th Anniversary Exhibit, 1970.** New York, New York Graphic Society, 1970.
Available - PPL 709.73 qN53n
Excellent photographs of 19th Century lighting.   Well documented.

Nutting, Wallace **Furniture Treasury (Mostly of American Origin). All Periods of American Furniture with Some Foreign Examples in America, also American Hardware and Household Utensils.** Framingham, Mass., Old America Company, 1928-1933. 3v.
Available - PPL R749 qN98 ft.
Many good photographs of lighting devices.

Pyne Press **Lamps and Other Lighting Devices.** Pyne Press Princeton, N.J., 1972
Available - GPL
Reproductions of catalogs of lighting devices published between 1850 and 1906.

Robins, F. W. **Story of the Lamp.** New York, Oxford Univ., Press, 1939.
Available - PPL 749 R657
History of the lamp from prehistoric times through the coming of electricity.   Photographs are of collections rather than of individual devices.

Roy, L. M. A. **Candle Book.** Brattleboro, Vermont, Stephen Daye, 1938.
Available - PPL 644.3 R88
Good photographs of early lighting devices, candle making, etc. shown with settings and costumes of period.

Rushlight Club **Early Lighting.** Rushlight Club, Boston, 1972.
Available - GPL

Thwing, Leroy Livingstone **Flickering Flames: a History of Domestic Lighting Through the Ages.** Rutland, Vermont, Tuttle, 1957.
Available - PPL 749 T54
History of lighting from classical times through 19th Century, with illustrations and glossary.

Watkins, Malcolm **Lamps of Colonial America.** (in Antiques, v. 32 no. 4, October 1937, pp. 187-191)
Available - PPL R050 A63 Art
Description and illustrations of early metal lighting devices.

Wyant, Major L. B. **Etiquette of 19th Century Lamps.** (in Antiques, v. 30 no. 3, September 1936, pp. 113-117)
Available - PPL R050 A63 Art
Article with contemporary quotations referring to particular types of lamps, their qualities and uses.

Yates, Raymond Francis and Yates, Marguerite W. **Guide to Victorian Antiques; with Notes on the Early Nineteenth Century.** New York, Harper, 1949.
Available - PPL 749 Y33g
Brief chapter on lights and lighting with illustrations.

FLOOR TREATMENTS

During the 17th century floors were generally left bare, and carpets were seldom used except as table coverings. By the mid-18th century many of the more pretentious houses had imported English or Oriental carpets, while the floors of more modest houses were usually painted, often in imitation of these imported carpets. Naturally finished floors, while favored by today's homeowners, were not typical of the 18th or 19th centuries. Although early hardwood floors were often waxed and polished, the more prevalent softwood floors were usually left bare or painted.

From colonial days to the mid-19th century, floor boards were thicker because the supporting beams were more widely spaced than is necessary today. Usually these boards were clear white pine about 1 1/8″ thick, preferably wide. The lesser quality boards were used in the attic, and these attics can be an excellent source of replacement boards today.

The boards were usually fastened with hand-wrought iron nails from the local blacksmith. In less expensive houses where the nailheads were left exposed, wear on the floor was uneven, leaving humps near the nailheads and hollows in the more heavily traveled areas. Better made floors had counterbored nails, plugged with a circular piece of wood which then wore down evenly with the rest of the floor. There are several sources today for hand-wrought nails — one is listed in the bibliography.

Many of the early floor treatments that follow are still practical and appropriate for old homes today. Whatever finishing method is selected, it is wise to delay floor finishing until all wall and ceiling plastering and painting is completed.

PAINTED FLOORS enriched the interiors of many country homes where fabric coverings were not available, though often these were embellished by some form of rug, carpeting or floorcloth. Often they were entirely covered with straw matting in the summer time, and colorful rag carpets in the winter months. In New England most floors were painted solid colors. Further research is in progress on colors used locally for plain painted floors. So far we have found varieties of gray, yellow ochre, dark red, brown, dark green and black.

Itinerant painters often undertook imitation woodgraining and painted floor patterns as well as wall decoration, moving from one house to another in a neighborhood. In areas of the room where these floors have been protected beneath furniture or later carpeting, traces of the old designs may still be quite clear. Patterns varied, but traditional diamonds, cubes, and squares, originally designed to simulate mosaic tile pavements, as in the Tate House in Stroudwater, appear to have been the most popular. Marbleized patterns also persisted over a long period and were sometimes used in conjunction with handsome scroll borders. In the 19th century they often appeared merely as random brush strokes, with the veining uncertain but still effective. During the Victorian period, checked or diamond patterns were particularly popular.

Freehand floor designs were occasionally reminiscent of English Turkey-fashion carpets. The Zalmon Bradley home in Fairfield, Connecticut, has such a design on the floor of an upper chamber. Apparently originally painted in salmon pink on a dark ground, the pigment of the figures was so heavily applied that it is still slightly raised above the surrounding surface.

STAIR RUNNER: Another procedure, practical as well as decorative, consisted of painting a figured strip down the middle of the front stairs and edging it with contrasting borders to give the appearance of a woven runner.

THE STENCILED FLOOR, which appeared after the Revolution and continued into the 1840's, was very popular and often quite colorful. The Joseph Lynde home in Melrose, Massachusetts, has a stenciled black design done in a gray ground on the parlor floor; there is also a stenciled pattern in yellow-green with a few units of medium brown done on an ochre background in the "northwest chamber." In the Ebenezer Waters home at West Sutton, Massachusetts, is a stenciled pattern of an eight-petaled flower in black done on a deep pumpkin ground. A home in Marblehead, Massachusetts, has black and gray octagons on a ground of dark green. This effect was achieved by first painting the floor green, then laying the octagons, probably with a stencil, and adding the gray details with another stencil. This leaves the centers of the octagons and the squares between the motifs in green, making an interesting combination in pattern and color.

Similar examples exist in Maine, and research is presently underway to document them.

Stenciled floors have a great variety of design, ranging from the simple conventionalized unit to the elaborate superimposed patterns, many of which can be found in books on stenciling. These designs pleased the eye, were practical, and took the place of the expensive inlaid floors of wood used in some of the early "ostentatious" dwellings, such as in the north parlor of the Clark-Frankland House built in Boston in 1715. Stenciled floors were also substitutes for "rich Persia carpets" and the more ordinary "stout carpeting", or for the "Painted Canvass Floor-Cloths" of the kind advertised in contemporary newspapers.

The method of stenciling floors was slightly more complicated than that of painting freehand. An excellent description of this process was published by

Rufus Porter, itinerant decorator, in his book **A Select Collection of Valuable and Curious Arts** in 1826: "Take a sheet of pasteboard or strongpaper, and paint thereon with a pencil any flower or figure that would be elegant for a border or carpet figure; then with small gouges and chissels, or a sharp pen knife, cut out the figure completely that is to be represented by aperatures through the paper. Lay this pattern on the ground intended to receive the figure, whether of floor or painted cloth, and with a still smoothe brush, paint with a quick vibrative motion over the whole figure. Then take up the paper and you will have an entire figure on the ground. If a floor is to be thus painted, in imitation of a carpet, the pattern must be perfectly square, and the figure so designed, that when several of them come together, they may completely match each other; and when different colors are used in the same figure, they must be kept a little separate from each other and wrought with different brushes."

SPATTER: Spatter finish appears to be a 19th century treatment and is very practical to use and repair today. The spatter-dash technique, a method of scattering drops of paint over a painted surface of another color, is relatively simple, and produces a colorful and authentic floor for a room of today. Practical "how-to-do-it" information appears in H. W. Congdon's book (see bibliography.)

Although painted floors were more subject to wear than woven carpets, they were easier to repair at home with good results and a minimum of expense. If one wishes to use a painted floor today, it is advisable to cover the paint with several coats of colorless dull urethane which, if renewed at proper intervals, will go far toward protecting the painted surface beneath.

As mentioned earlier, natural floor boards were not held in the same high esteem as they are today. It appears that more formal rooms were, in fact, painted as soon as paint was readily available and time permitted. However, it is probably true that less formal rooms continued to have unpainted floors much longer. For those who like the effect of "natural boards", there are many different formulas available, several of which are on file at GPL. Information is also available in H. L. and O. Williams' book (see bibliography) on how to treat wide cracks between boards, which is a particular problem where the temperature and humidity of the room vary widely with the seasons, as in Maine.

Regardless of the final finish decided upon, it is essential that old softwood planks not be robbed of their patina by the use of a drum or disc sander which can leave permanent circular scars, and can produce a perfectly flat characterless surface robbed forever of its special charm. Though time consuming, hand scraping is often a much more satisfactory solution. In addition, paint remover, steel wool, and light sanding, either by hand or very carefully with an orbital sander, are useful techniques, which produce a more pleasing surface.

Some varieties of wood used in old floors may not sand well and may splinter excessively. If this is the case, the more typical painted surface or an appropriate floor covering would be the most satisfactory solution. Removing and/or turning damaged or warped boards is considered risky, but the technical problems involved are discussed thoroughly in the Williams' book. (see bibliography.)

We would particularly appreciate hearing of any local examples of floor colors and stencil designs in Maine which have not yet been documented and which you may unearth in your own restoration.

BIBLIOGRAPHY

Comstock, Helen (Editor) **Concise Encyclopedia of American Antiques.** N.Y., Hawthorne, 1958.
    Available - PPL R749 C73 Art

Congdon, H. W. **Early American Homes for Today; a Treasury of Decorative Details and Restoration Procedures.** Rutland, Vermont, Tuttle, 1963. Second printing, 1969.
    Available - GPL
        - PPL 728 qC74e
    Good practical information on refinishing, spatter-dash, etc.

French, Leigh, Jr. **Colonial Interiors, First Series; Photographs and Measured Drawings of the Colonial and Early Federal Periods.** New York, W. Helburn, 1923.
    Available - PPL R728 qF87

Little, Nina Fletcher **American Decorative Wall Painting 1700-1850.** Sturbridge, Mass., Old Sturbridge Village, 1952. New enlarged edition, New York, Dutton, 1972.
    Available - GPL 1972 ed.
        - PPL 1972 ed. 747 qL77 1972
    Also discusses floor treatment

Little, Nina Fletcher **Floor Coverings in New England Before 1850.** Sturbridge, Mass., Old Sturbridge Village, 1967. Pamphlet.
    Available - GPL

Roth, Rodris **Floor Coverings in Eighteenth Century America.** Washington, D.C., Smithsonian Institution Press, 1967. Pamphlet.
    Available - GPL

Waring, Janet **Early American Stencils on Walls and Furniture.** New York, W. R. Scott, 1937. New York, Dover reprint 1968.
    Available - GPL Dover reprint
        - PPL 1937 ed. R747 qW27 also circulating copy

Williams, Henry Lionel and Williams, Ottalie **Old American Houses 1700-1850. How to Restore, Remodel and Reproduce Them.** New York, Bonanza, 1957.
    Available - GPL
    Excellent and valuable "how-to" information

BOOKLETS

Floor Coverings in New England Before 1850 Pub: Old Sturbridge Village, 1967
    Sturbridge, Massachusetts 01566

Old House Journal. Vol. II, no. 5, May 1974. Practical "how-to" information on repairing sagging floors, damaged floorboards, cracks between boards, and other problems.
    Available - GPL

Old House Journal. Vol. II no. 12, Dec. 1974. Very detailed instructions on sanding, removal of old glue from linoleum covering, practical information on removal of old finishes.
    Available - GPL

Booklet, 22 pages, available for 10c from Pierce & Stevens Chemical Corp, P.O. Box 1092, Buffalo, New York, 14240:

"How to Finish Wood Floors". Easy to follow guidance on sanding, scraping, floor finishes, etc. Recommended by "Old House Journal."

Tremont Nail Company, 21 Elm Street, P.O. Box 111, Wareham, Mass. 02571. A good source for colonial style nails, manufactured according to authentic old patterns. Sample kit of 20 patterns available, including a history of nails in America for $3.00.

Finishing Touches:
    A collection of recipes for finishing wood.
    Pub: 1963: Obtainable from the
    National Trust for Historic Preservation, 740-748 Jackson Place, N.W., Washington, D.C. 20006

PAINT

With the advent in recent years of a reverence for the look of "natural wood" in old buildings, attention to research into the history of paint use and color has been somewhat neglected. There is a growing interest, however, in authenticity with regard to restoration. This has led to more complex research techniques in all aspects of restoration including the subject of paint. There is also a recent movement which encourages preservation as opposed to restoration, particularly with regard to early buildings other than museums. Thus, preservation techniques are now being studied for the purpose of retaining as many as possible of the physical aspects of a building which show its growth and change through its whole lifetime.

RESEARCH

There is little evidence that paint was used at all in this country in the years before 1725. The efforts of early Americans had to be directed toward survival in the 17th and 18th centuries, and this left little opportunity for the more refined aspects of living. By the middle of the 18th century however, most city houses and some in outlying areas had both exterior and interior paint. (It is a common misconception that the exteriors of frame houses were left uncolored in the 18th and subsequent centuries.) Interiors were painted with brightly colored whitewash and distemper, while oil paint was used infrequently. The oil medium when used was usually linseed, but could be other vegetable oils, or even fish oil.

Early colors were obtained most often by grinding and mixing powdered pigment with lime as a medium. Pigments usually derived from two categories: natural earths, which are actually iron oxide or silicate; or synthetic or manufactured compounds of metal such as lead white, prussian blue, or lampblack.

Whitewash was in common use for covering plaster walls. Many early recipes have been found for it. It usually consisted of a mixture of lime and water, often with whiting (chalk powder) or glue size added.

Distemper was another early type of paint. The powdered color (pigment) was mixed with glue size, water, oil, or whatever medium was being used to bind the pigment together and make it spreadable. Chalk provided white, which was often used as a primer coat under distemper colors in the nineteenth century. White distemper was considered the most elegant paint for ceilings and walls, but moisture caused it to crack, peel, and bubble.

Eighteenth century colors were mostly strong and dark; some of the more popular being Indian red, yellow ochre, indigo blue, Spanish brown, green, and gray. Popular exterior colors of this time were white, red, green and yellow, with trim usually done in white and doors in black, green, and blue.

The practice of glazing over interior colors for the purpose of achieving a look of depth and sheen was widely used in the 18th century. Graining and marbleizing also began to be done in these early years. Glazes were made from mixtures consisting primarily of linseed oil with some white lead or a small amount of pigment added, and sometimes chalk as well. The graining which was done in the 18th century differed from the later style in its large sweeping strokes done with a brush.

Another painting practice mentioned in connection with this century was that of painting brick exteriors red and penciling in the mortar joints, sometimes to coincide with the real joints and sometimes not.

The 19th century brought about some refinements in painting as well as in the other decorative arts. One innovation which occurred shortly after the turn of the century was the introduction of milk-based or casein paint. Milk was an easily obtainable substitute for oil as a paint vehicle and many recipes for milk paints can be found in accounts dated around 1800. This type of paint was suitable only for interior use, however, since it would not withstand the effects of weather.

The practice of graining continued to be popular in the 19th century and gradually came to be more of a literal simulation of various types of wood achieved by the use of a graining comb instead of a brush.

Much decorative work was done during the early 1800's by itinerant artists like Rufus Porter and Moses Eaton, two who were noted for their work in the New England area. Their contributions to interior painting ranged from simple stenciled border designs to large whole-wall paintings.

During the Classical Revival years after 1830 it became popular to use softer, more subtle colors. Plaster friezes and medallions were often tinted in delicate shades. A variety of colors was sometimes used in the same room; for example, paneling might be done in two shades of blue, the moulding in imitation bronze or gold leaf, a plaster frieze in blue, purple and gray, the ceiling in light blue, and the walls in a soft gray.

Exteriors in the Greek Revival period were mostly white or soft stone colors. Around 1850 some references can be found to a simulated stone finish for exteriors. This effect was achieved by mixing sand with the paint.

There were, in the mid 1800's, still frequent references to wood graining, and as the century wore on, more frequent use of marbleized slate was noted. This look of marble was achieved by dropping pigment in oil onto a surface of water, stirring it about, and then lowering the slate face down onto this surface. The results were so good that it was sometimes impossible to tell simulated marble from the real.

Prepared paints became available in this country in 1858, but did not come into general use until after the Civil War. By this time a wide variety of colors was readily available and people were no longer limited in their choices. The Victorian period, from the 1850's to the end of the century, saw many variations in uses of paint colors and combinations. In addition to painted surfaces, varnished woodwork came into vogue in the Victorian era. This was the famous "golden oak" period, but in addition to the oak many other types of wood were used, or suggested by graining.

Victorian period colors appear better and brighter because they are more recent. However, 18th century colors generally were originally clearer and brighter, often with less sheen than the later paints. Light has dimmed some pigments, especially prussian blue, and the fresh effect of some has been yellowed by chemical changes in the oil over-gloss applied to give the colors depth and sheen.

RESTORATION

The techniques used in interior paint restoration are far beyond the average homeowner's capabilities. It is possible to try to reproduce the look of early paint by grinding dry pigment and mixing it with linseed oil. But the pleasing variations in color resulting from poor dispersion of pigments, and the appearance of depth acquired from the use of glazes, would be difficult to achieve without museum techniques. Therefore, it is best and easiest to use a commercially produced paint which closely matches an original color found in the building, or an appropriate color pleasing to the owners. Most paint companies offer a "restoration line" copied from such projects as Williamsburg, Newport, and Sturbridge. Many paint dealers are helpful in trying to match a particular color with their tinting shades. Uncertainty of the effect of a particular color can be resolved by painting a sample on a large piece of white paper or board and placing it **in situ.**

PRESERVATION

In order to preserve handsome paint in an old building, ideally, of course, it should not be removed. However, this is impractical in most cases for private homeowners.

If some preservation of original paint is undertaken, an "isolating layer" should be used over it. The material for this should be appropriate to the paint underneath, a decision best made by a professional paint conservator. Two of the pitfalls thus avoided are progressively yellowing varnishes, and protective coats which cannot be removed without damage to original paint. A conservator would be able to suggest alternatives. The best place to leave old paint intact when repainting is around doorways, windows, and especially hardware. Then if analysis is someday attempted, lumps of the old paint can be dug out to be professionally examined with sophisticated techniques. If it is not feasible to uncover and retain original paint, a small area of progressive layers of old paint can be neatly exposed in an inconspicuous part of the room, thus adding to the knowledge and enjoyment of the building's interior history.

Exterior paint, on the other hand, seems best preserved by a cover of new paint which will weather away with time and so prevent early colors from peeling off in one piece along with the top coat. For Victorian frame exterior colors A. J. Downing (in an article noted in the bibliography) dislikes white and lists appropriate colors and how they are mixed.

BIBLIOGRAPHY

Allen, Eugene **Analytical Color Matching.** (in Journal of Paint Technology, v. 39, June 1967, pp. 368-376) Association for Preservation Technology.
  Paint Color Research and House Painting Practices. (in A P T Newsletter, v. 1, no. 2, August 1969, pp. 1-19).
  Available - GPL

Batcheler, Penelope H. **Paint Color Research and Restoration.** (American Association for State and Local History, Technical Leaflet No. 15, published as part of History News, v. 23 no. 10, October 1968.)
  Available - GPL

Brommelle, Norman **Colour and Conservation.** (in Studies in Conservation II, October 1955, pp. 76-85)

Candee, Richard M. **Housepaints in Colonial America, Their Materials, Manufacture, and Application.** (in Color Engineering. Chromatic Publishing Company)

Candee, Richard M. **Rediscovery of Milk-based House Paints and the Myth of "Brickdust and Buttermilk" Paints.** (in Old Time New England, v. 58 no. 3, January-March 1968, Serial no. 211, pp. 79-81)
  Available - GPL
        - PPL R974 S67 Art

Downing, A. J. "**Downing on Color**". (In The Old House Journal. October 1974, p. 11.)

Gardner, F. B. **The Carriage Painters' Illustrated Manual.** New York; S. R. Wells & Co. 1880.
  Available - PPL 684 G22
  This book and the one titled Hints and Practical Information for Cabinet-Makers...etc. are full of hints, methods, and recipes for painting and removing paint and varnish from metal, wood, and painting tools. They are out-of-date in places but make fascinating reading.

Gettens, Rutherford John and Stout, George L. **Painting Materials, a Short Encyclopedia.** New York, Van Nostrand, 1942. New York, Dover reprint, 1965.
  Available - PPL 751 G39

Johnston, Ruth M. **Spectrophotometry for the Analysis and Description of Color.** (in Journal of Paint Technology, v. 39, June 1967)

Johnston, Ruth M. and Feller, Robert L. **Use of Differential Spectral Curve Analysis in the Study of Museum Objects.** (Reprint from Dyestuffs, v. 44, December 1963. New York, Allied Chemical)

Little, Nina Fletcher **American Decorative Wall Painting 1700-1850.** Sturbridge, Mass., Old Sturbridge Village, 1952. New enlarged edition, New York, Dutton, 1972.
  Available - GPL 1972 ed.
        - PPL 1972 ed. 747 qL77 1972

Nash, Susan H. **Paints, Furniture and Furnishings. The Restoration of Colonial Williamsburg in Virginia.** (in Architectural Record, v. 78, December 1935, pp. 447-449)
  Available - GPL

Phillips, Morgan W. "**Problems in the Restoration and Preservation of Old Paints.**" A paper presented at Williamsburg in 1974.
  Available - GPL

Phillips, Morgan and Whitney, Christopher **Restoration of Original Paints at Otis House.** (in Old Time New England, v. 62, no. 1, July-Sept. 1971, Serial no. 225, pp. 25-28)
  Available - GPL
        - PPL R974 s67 Art

Phin, John **Hints and Practical Information for Cabinet-makers, Upholsterers, and Furniture Men Generally.** New York; Fred A. Hodgson, 1884.
  Available - PPL 698.1 p. 57

Whiffen, Marcus **Eighteenth-Century Houses of Williamsburg; a Study of Architecture and Building in the Colonial Capital of Virginia.** New York, Holt, Rinehart and Winston, 1960. p. 15 for **Paint**
  Available - GPL
        - PPL 728 qw57

WALLPAPER

One of the last but none the less exciting decisions you may be making in the restoration of your old house is a choice of interior wall treatment.

It is particularly important to remember that the age, geographical location and the economic status of its former occupant will have a direct bearing on the type of treatment which would have been used. Perhaps your choice would be made easier by knowing (1) what would have been appropriate at that time, (2) what was in the house, (3) what is available today and (4) books for further research.

Various methods were used to finish walls at different periods, ranging from the plain plastered surface with wood sheathing of the early periods to the painted murals and stencils of the mid-19th century. Local examples of such treatments are being studied by the Advisory Service. The following article will deal only with wallpaper.

DEVELOPMENT OF WALLPAPER

1750 - 1850: HAND PRINTED ERA

The first European wallpaper was made in imitation of costly tapestries, hangings of painted cloth, leather and wood paneling. Large formal patterns including the favorite pineapple or artichoke designs were printed on paper in imitation of the Florentine and Genoese cut velvets. This early paper was called "Flocked Paper" and was made by printing the design on the paper in glue or varnish and scattering chopped wool over all. The wool would adhere to the glue and form the design. Although flocked paper was being made as early as 1620 in France it did not become popular until the English perfected it and produced it from 1720 - 1750. It was advertised in this country but little evidence of flocked paper remains. Any paper seen at this time would have been imported since the first manufacturing of wallpaper in this country was by Plunket Fleeson in 1739, in Philadelphia.

By the end of the 17th century Chinese Papers were being imported into Europe through the East India Companies. They typically depicted Chinese scenes and designs. They were quickly imitated, along with Chinese motifs on other forms of decorative arts, hence the term "chinoiserie."

Wallpaper begins to become more common in American homes by 1750, replacing plastered or paneled walls. Imported papers were copied here, both figured and plain; blue was a favored color, along with green, pink and orange. Sometimes mica was applied to the paper for a glittering effect.

Some of the advertisements of the day indicate the latest styles. "A very extensive assortment of papers from quarter of a dollar per piece upward. Also, a stock of 4,000 pieces of French Paper, from lowest priced to the most superb patterns, with a variety of land scape pieces wanted for fireboards and boarders." Some of these examples have been preserved. They are in the classical style, typical of the period.

Around 1800 the importation of French papers surpasses that of the English. The Americans copied the French designs of toile such as pastoral scenes and small vase and floral motifs. Striped papers, papers with geometrical designs, architectural decorations, and imitations of statuary were usual, as were papers imitating paneling and marble. These would also have related dadoes and fringes, bottom to top. There were commemorative papers, some made in this country and some in France, depicting American heroes and battles. Papers imitating fabric of satin, lace and damask hung in folds, were seen. The colors of bright greens, glaring yellows, violet, strong oranges and reds and blues, plus contrasting black and white were prevalent.

The 1820's saw designs of simple flowers or imitation damask in blue, green and yellow colors. The papers were printed in continuous rolls, and seams are seldom found after this date.

By 1830 an eclecticism of style appears in response to European preferences. The Cathedral style seen in France depicted church interiors and pointed archways and leaded windows. A bit later the French turn to illustrating the 16th century with scenes of the chase, strolling couples and gardens. Elaborate panel decorations were being produced in France but in this country simpler variations were used. A general deterioration of styles was seen in England at this time. Popular motifs were strap work decorations. Relief effects were sought by imitating stucco and wood moldings.

A revolt against over-elaborate style started the trend toward Gothic style in its pure form.

French papers were an imporant influence in decorating homes during the whole of the eighteenth century. Papillon and Reveillon were important names in the manufacture of French wallpaper, some of which was imported into this country and copied. One reason for the popularity of the French papers around 1800 was the rage for scenic papers which were meant to encircle a room without repetitions. One wood block was needed for each color or shade in each design and so thousands of wood blocks were required. Typical scenes depicted romantic landscapes, views of countries or cities, historical scenes showing conquest, adventure or mythology, literary or hunting and racing scenes. In the case of Dufours' "Voyages of Captain Cook" he supplied the purchaser with instructions for hanging the paper in proper sequence, and explained the scenes depicted in the paper. These papers were imported, mainly in New England, for the next forty years. In fact, there are more French scenic papers found in this country than in France.

Since these papers were quite expensive and often took a year to complete, it was not usual to find much free-hand printing.

Painting on paper rather than walls had an advantage, since the paper was first glued to a canvas which was then tacked onto a wooden frame attached to the wall.

Fireboard papers were a part of the wallpaper industry until 1850. These boards covered the fireplace opening when there was no fire. The papers were often in scenes, landscapes or vases of flowers. The **trompe l'oeil** or "fool the eye" fireboard papers were sometimes used.

There were papers made to go just over a doorway. These were usually done in panels showing famous paintings.

Borders are mentioned along with the papers themselves. They were an important part of the decoration of wallpaper and the early papers were made with the border as part of the wallpaper. Later they were made to be applied separately. It is known that in 1765, Benjamin Franklin had his parlor papered in plain blue with a "gilt border". These early borders were of one or two inch width. Most papers had borders, although some like the arch and pillar papers did not.

By 1780 the newspapers advertised festooned borders which feature designs of swags or ribbons and ropes of roses or other flowers. These could be used with plain or patterned papers. Some borders had a straight edge and others were meant to be cut to follow a curve in the pattern before hanging. They were seen along chair-rails, cornices, around window, door and mantel pieces. Ceiling decorations of papier-mache to simulate stucco were in evidence. By 1790 the so-called jumbo borders often filled the entire space below the rail. In 1800, the borders imitated costly materials and embroidery designs. Materials of satin, lace and damask would seem to be "draped" in heavy folds or swags. In 1813 the newspapers offer English and American papers of small landscapes, drapery and other figures and many common borders showing yellow silk damask, moreens, handsome ball and common fringes. In 1825 paper of damask satin showing rich cloth borders and marble is seen.

1850 - 1900: INFLUENCE OF THE MACHINE

The first color printing machine was imported to this country from Europe by John Howell of Philadelphia for his factory in 1844. Instead of using wood blocks, printing was done by rollers or cylinders. Large amounts of paper could be printed since endless or continuous paper had been invented in England. As a result of machine printing, the scale of pattern was reduced and the colors became thinner. The paper also became brittle as fewer rags and more wood pulp was used in production.

By 1860 the rococo revival taste in wallpaper is seen in the use of naturalistic flowers. Flocked paper made an appearance again, produced in deep reds, dark green or blues, in exaggerated damask design. Gilded papers were seen at this time also.

54

In 1862 William Morris in England rebelled against the many cheap machine papers being produced by issuing through the Jeffrey Company his Trellis Paper. It was done in vegetable dyes and wood blocks. He was a master of design and color and many of his papers are well known. They were popular in America. He brought new appreciation of the possibilities of wallpaper and he influenced furniture designers as well. Nature was his inspiration.

During the 1870's the English influence took over the trade magazines and the "Aesthetic Movement" was emphasized. Japanese influence was seen in asymmetrical designs, and the sunflower, Egyptian and Moorish themes became popular. New ways to use the machine were explored; border, frieze and dado designs were seen. The damask and drawing room style papers with contrast between matt print and a shiny ground also appeared at this time. Papers with a glittering surface caused by mixing mica in the ground as well as in the paint were introduced. A technique invented in 1877 of coloring the paper in the pulp enabled papers to be washed. These were the first sanitary papers.

We are continuing to document local examples and you are urged to contact the Advisory Service concerning your finds.

The following was taken from an Association For Preservation Technology Newsletter article by Mrs. Catherine Lynn Frangiamore, Curator, Atlanta Historical Society, formerly with the Cooper-Hewitt Museum. We thank her for her permission to use it.

WHAT TO DO WHEN OLD WALLPAPER IS DISCOVERED DURING THE INVESTIGATION OF A STRUCTURE

1. Even before you FIND it, when working on a restoration project in an old house, particularly a 19th century house, know WHERE to look for the various kinds of wallpaper and borders which may have been used in combination within the same room. Look for border papers around doors and windows, and around mantels. Look for them at chair-rail, base-board, and frieze levels. Frequently, dado, side-wall fill, and frieze patterns of different patterns were used together. If you find a sample of a border somewhere in a room, don't assume that was the only border used. Check to be sure that there are no traces of use of another border or of that same border around all edges of woodwork trimming. On ceilings, look for wallpaper corners and borders, as well as for ornamental centers. Before you strip down walls, check all over them for long-since layered over evidence of early, perhaps complex uses and combinations of patterns and borders.

2. Record what you find. Photograph fragments in color before you try to remove them, and keep accurate records of where on the walls or ceilings the papers were found, by drawing plans of the rooms and elevations of the walls and ceilings.

3. Try to remove the samples intact and preserve them.

Not too infrequently, old papers will simply come right off with a little gentle sliding of a spatula, palette knife, etc., under the papers, because the old glue will have dried out and lost its adhesive qualities. Try to get a flat blade under the papers as this gentle disturbance of the glue may release the papers without enormous effort.

At the other extreme, sometimes fragile old papers are found glued tight as can be right on unfinished boards. Any attempts to pry the papers loose will destroy them, so the obvious thing to do is to remove the board and save the whole thing.

Most frequently the application of a little moisture to soften the old wallpaper paste will be sufficient to get the samples off a wall in a reasonable state of preservation. I prefer to steam the paste to moisten it so I can remove the paper. I have successfully used a small hand-held steamer, such as those currently marketed at most hardware stores for home-and-travel-steaming of clothes. In buying a steamer, be sure to get one with a head that produces a line or a point of steam that can be concentrated on a limited area. In using a steamer, you are trying to wet the glue, not the paper, (though the paper is obviously going to absorb some of the moisture) so try to start your steaming in a corner or other point where the paper is already loose, and where you can direct the jet of steam under the paper right at the glue. Sometimes this isn't possible, and you have to start by pointing the steamer straight at the paper, but as soon as possible, peel the paper away from the wall and direct the steam at the paste. As you steam, have a piece of screening (wire window screening with the edges protectively covered with masking tape) to "catch" and support the paper as you remove it from the vertical wall. Instead of wire screening, sometimes a blotter will do. The operation is easier with two people... one to steam and one to support the paper as it comes off the wall.

If you have multi-layers of paper, it is unpredictable how they will come off. It's easiest to first remove the whole "sandwich" of layered papers and steam them apart afterwards when you can lay them flat on a table, and not have to fight gravity as you remove sagging wet layers from a vertical wall. I prefer steaming layers apart, because most wallpaper pigments are water soluble, and I seem to get less color fading using steam rather than soaking the layers apart.

Abbott Lowell Cummings at the SPNEA has successfully for many years separated layers of wallpaper by having them soaked in a large flat pan of lukewarm water. Once you put the papers in water, keep a close watch. They should not soak too long, or the paper will become pulpy. As soon as the glue begins to melt, which fortunately happens before the colors start running, in most cases, have a piece of wire screening ready to slide under the top-most layer, to act as a supportive draining tray for removing the layers one by one. They can be carried on this tray to a surface for drying. Sometimes blotter paper will do, if the glue has been mostly washed away. Waxed paper, tin foil, or a screen will do for a supportive surface while the paper is drying.

As most wallpaper pigments are water soluble, you can expect some color fading, whether you steam or soak them. That's the biggest reason to try to get good color photographs of samples before you try to get them off the wall.

In some cases, non-water-soluble glues are used. Use various solvents on Q-tips to test until you find the solvent that will melt the particular glue that might have been used. Moistening the glue will then have to be done with cotton or a cloth for the solvent and steaming will be impossible for such non-water soluble glues.

4. If you find large areas of particularly old paper in good condition (as sometimes show up under wood paneling applied at a later date), a paper which could be re-used in a restored room, or a scenic paper which might have market value, call a professional paper or painting conservationist. If they can remove and remount frescoes, they can work their chemical juggling magic in removing and remounting large areas of wallpaper. This is, however, too specialized and difficult a job for amateurs. If you think you have an unusually fine wall full of paper, check with experts before you ruin it.

5. I think that the best way to preserve small samples of wallpaper is to treat them as if they were prints and to mat them on good stiff 4-ply mat boards so that they will be supported by a rigid surface. This is not what is done with wallpapers in a number of well-known collections, but for small delicate samples, I think it's the best way to protect them, and allow them to be displayed temporarily by simply putting the pre-matted samples in standard sized frames. They can be stored as prints in Solander boxes, made of acid-free materials which will not damage the paper. I would suggest **not** putting these samples on display, but if you want to display them, be sure to protect them from color-fading and other deterioration by keeping them out of bright light and using ultra-violet filtering plexiglas in framing.

6. In order to have a reproduction made of the wallpaper, you should be sure to preserve a minimum of a full width and a complete repeat of any pattern you might find. Widths are usually under 22″ and repeat lengths normally are under 36″. If you have duplicates, even if you cannot mount them properly, it is helpful to colleagues and researchers, if you send your duplicate samples to a museum collection where records of wallpaper used in 18th and 19th century interiors are kept. In sending such samples to museums, it is helpful if you duplicate all available information about the house.

SOURCES

Most companies listed below have showrooms in Boston at 420 Boylston Street, Boston, Massachusetts 02116. They can be visited by the trade or by those with a letter of introduction from an Account. These companies carry documentary or period design papers and many reproduce wallpapers for restorations around the country.

The companies starred carry companion fabrics. Order through interior designers or other outlets.

* Katzenbach and Warren Inc. - also distributes the Dorothy Waterhouse Collection.
* F. Schumacher and Co.
* Greeff Fabrics, Inc.
* Old Stone Mill Corporation, Grover Street, Adams, Mass. 01220.
* Thomas Strahan. Thomas Strahan Co., Chelsea, Mass. 02150.
  Jones and Erwin
  Only interior designers carry these samples:
* Brunschwig and Fils.
* Scalamandré
  Clarance House
* A. L. Diament and Co., 2415 Sath St., Philadelphia, Pa. 19146.
  Nancy McClelland Inc., 232 East 59 St., N.Y., N.Y. 10022.

BIBLIOGRAPHY

Ackerman, Phyllis **Wallpapers from Old New England Houses** (in Antiques: V. 59 no. 5, May 1956, pp. 440-443.)
   Available - GPL - PPL

Hotchkiss, Horace L. **"Wallpapers used in America 1700-1850"**, (In The Concise Encyclopedia of American Antiques, edited by Helen Comstock - Hawthorn, 1958. pp. 760-768.)
   Available - PPL R749 C73 Art.

Katzenbach, Lois and Katzenbach, William **Practical Book of American Wallpaper.** Phila., Pa., Lippincott, 1951.
   Available - PPL R745 qK192.
   A history of wallpaper with pictures showing old and comtemporary designs.

McClelland, Nancy Vincent **Historical Wallpapers, from Their Inception to the Introduction of Machinery.** Phila., Pa., Lippincott, 1924.
   Available - PPL R745 qM12.
   A general history of wallpaper development and styles up to machine printing. Many plates.

Sanborn, Katherine Abbott **Old Time Wall Papers; an Account of the Pictorial Papers on Our Forefathers' Walls, with a Study of Their Historical Development.** New York, Literary Collector Press, 1905. New York, Dover reprint.
   Available - PPL 745 qS19 & circ. copy.
   Many plates are shown esp. of the scenic wallpapers. A brief history is included.

Sugden, Alan Victor and Edmondson, John Ludlam **History of English Wallpaper,** 1509-1914. New York, Scribner's, 1925.
   Available - PPL R745 fS94.
   Lovely color plates.

58

WALL PAINTINGS

In the beginning of this country's existence a generally puritanical outlook made the use of interior paint seem ostentatious, and interiors were not as gay as they were to become.

The Revolution changed the lives of many Americans. Material progress and improved communications contributed to the desire for more colorful interiors and ornamentation. The frescoes and stenciled walls that may still be found in some of our early houses were an expression of this desire to beautify domestic surroundings. The imported wallpapers of the more well-to-do were the inspiration for many of these decorations.

Wall painting flourished at the beginning of the nineteenth century, perhaps because the improvement of the roads allowed more freedom to travel. Journeymen painters traveling about the countryside with their simple equipment (dry colors for mixing their paints, heavy oiled paper for their stencils, a sharp knife for cutting, and a few measuring tools) became a common sight. These itinerant painters, for room and board and a small wage, would transform the plain walls of a room into brightly colored design.

One painter whose stenciling has been well documented is Moses Eaton, from New Hampshire, who traveled extensively throughout Maine where many examples of his work are still in existence. His original stenciling kit, now owned by the Society for the Preservation of New England Antiquities, discovered in an attic, contains not only everyday tools, but stencils still intact, which can serve the house restorer. Nina Fletcher Little's and Janet Waring's books have fine illustrations of his work.

The name most frequently associated with freehand wall painting is Rufus Porter. Although his family lived in Portland, Maine, he spent a lifetime traveling throughout New England. Many of his beautiful frescoes and painted panels remain. A list of those found in Maine is in Jean Lipman's book entitled **Rufus Porter, A Yankee Pioneer.** The initials of Porter's nephew, Jonathan Poor, have also appeared in Maine houses.

Other documented interior painters and those as yet unrecognized, make reasonable the assumption that local as well as itinerant artisans tried their hand at these decorative arts. Even the homeowner could obtain stencils to try his own hand at executing designs.

STENCILING is the painting of a variety of motifs on a flat surface using a heavy oiled or painted paper with a cut out pattern. The pattern is either drawn or traced on the paper and then cut out with a sharp knife. Paint is applied to the cut out areas with a stiff brush. The designs are usually arranged in a repetitious manner. Popular motifs were flowers, fruit, foliage and birds along with many geometric designs.

FRESCO is painting on a wet or moist plaster wall. Today the term fresco is generally used to describe all types of old wall decorative painting. Like overmantels, frescoes were usually scenic murals of local surroundings.

OVERMANTEL is the decoration of the area over the fireplace, which naturally became a focus of attention. Often a local landscape, sometimes including the owner's house, was the decorative feature; at other times an imaginary scene occupied the area.

FIREBOARDS designed to cover the fireplace in the warmer months were usually wood or canvas stretched on a frame. Generally, these seem to have been ornamented by the painter who decorated the rest of the room. Like overmantels the fireboards served as a visual focal point during the time they were in use.

There must be many houses with beautiful wall paintings or stenciling yet to be discovered, perhaps hidden under many layers of wallpaper. Imagine the excitement of such a find! Everyone recognizes the value of a primitive painting that you hang on a wall but until recently only a relatively few knowledgeable people appreciated the fact that those applied directly to the wall were of equal value and interest. This lack of appreciation has led to the destruction of many handsomely decorated walls and has contributed to the loss of valuable folk art. If you are one of the fortunate few to make such a discovery, preservation should be foremost in your mind. This would be the time to get in touch with us. Many techniques have been discussed, technology is ever changing, and we will be happy to assist you in the procedures best suited to your preservation needs. Research and recording of stencils and wall paintings are being carried out at Greater Portland Landmarks, and newly discovered local examples are important to our continuing study.

BIBLIOGRAPHY

Allen, Edward B. **Early American Wall Paintings 1710-1850.** New Haven, Connecticut, Yale University Press, 1926.
    Available - GPL
    Some Maine examples are included in this study of American frescoes and stencils.

Brazer, Esther Stevens **Basic Instructions for Home Painting in the Early American Manner.** New York, Clarence W. Brazer, 1945.
    Available - GPL
          - PPL 745 B82b
    As its title suggests, a small handbook with basic instructions. Chapter V, pp. 21-25 covers preparation of walls, background paint, pattern selection and cutting instructions for stenciling walls and floors.

Brazer, Esther Stevens **Early American Decoration.** Springfield, Massachusetts, Pond-Ekberg Company, 1940.
    Available - PPL R745 qB82
    A limited section pertinent to our subject. Part 15, pp. 167-171. These pages cover paint selection, design planning, for stenciled as well as freehand wall painting. Part 15 is preceded by several photographs of stenciled walls and floors.

Lipman, Jean **American Folk Decoration.** New York, Oxford University Press, 1951, New York, Dover reprint 1972.
Available - PPL 745.4 qL76
Chapter 5, "Architectural Decoration", includes instructions for planning, preparation, and execution of wall stencils. Figure 128, page 102, is a Moses Eaton pattern available for copying.

Lipman, Jean **American Primitive Painting.** New York, Oxford University Press, 1942, New York, Dover reprint 1972.
Available - PPL R759.1 qL76
One chapter on wall decorations including photographs of frescoes and painted panels, pp. 121-138.

Lipman, Jean **Rufus Porter, Yankee Pioneer.** New York, Clarkson N. Potter, Inc., 1968.
Available - GPL
- PPL R747 q84L Me. coll. also circ.
A definitive study of the life and works of Rufus Porter; a man of many and varied talents with a picturesque career. Enjoyable reading for all. Porter was particularly well known for his frescoes and this book has beautiful pictures of many.

Lipman, Jean and Winchester, Alice **The Flowering of American Folk Art (1776-1876).** New York, The Viking Press Inc., 1974.
Available - PPL R709.73 qL76f & also circulating copy.
pp. 190-213 includes information on overmantels, fireboards, and stencils with equally important color and black and white plates.

Little, Nina Fletcher **American Decorative Wall Painting 1700-1850.** Sturbirdge, Massachusetts, Old Sturbridge Village, 1952. New enlarged edition, New York, Dutton, 1972.
Available - GPL 1972 ed.
- PPL 747 qL77 1972
An excellent book from cover to cover. Text and photographs are exceptional. A biographical list of painters is included. A must for anyone with an interest in decorative wall painting.

Peterson, Harold L. **Americans at Home.** New York, Charles Scribner's Sons, 1971.
Available - GPL
A collection of paintings depicting domestic interiors, which is another valuable resource for students of wall painting. Backgrounds will often show popular wall treatments of the times.

Sabine, Ellen S. **Early American Decorative Patterns.** D. Van Nostrand Company Inc., 1962.
Available - PPL 745.4 qS11e
Chapter II, pp. 56-68, contains step by step instructions for the amateur home painter along with a collection of authentic pattern designs for copying.

Waring, Janet **Early American Stencils on Walls and Furniture.** New York, W. R. Scott, 1937. New York, Dover reprint 1968.
Available - GPL
- PPL 1937 ed. R747 qW27
Entire book an invaluable reference. It contains a detailed history of stenciling as well as many fine photographs of New England examples.

HOUSE HARDWARE

LATE EIGHTEENTH THROUGH MID-NINETEENTH CENTURY

During this period thumb latches were in general use on country houses. Surface mounted spring latches (with oval or round solid brass knobs, and keyhole-shaped or square-shaped backplate) and box locks were found on some of the better buildings. Wrought-iron bolts were used for added security.

Surface mounted H or HL hinges were common on interior doors until the 1820's although the heavy cast-iron butt hinge comes in around 1800. These were sometimes mounted on the face of the door at first, later on the jamb edge.

Many forms of wrought-iron strap hinges were used on shutters and exterior doors, some batten doors and on outbuildings. These continued to be used into the twentieth century. By the 1860's cast-iron versions of this hinge were available.

The simplest form of thumb latch is the wrought-iron Suffolk latch, usually having the familiar Bean or Arrow-shaped cusps which give it its name. The earliest type has the thumb press passing through the cusp; later it is made to pass through the neck of the latch immediately below the cusp. This is the type more commonly found in Maine.

The Suffolk latch overlaps in period the later more elaborate Norfolk latch, which has a rolled sheet-iron backplate. An early version of this (appearing around 1800) has a cast-iron backplate and is usually very plain. The later latches have many variations in their backplate and pull; the pull is sometimes trimmed with pewter in the more elaborate ones. Much of this hardware was imported in large quantities from blacksmiths in England who specialized in making latches and house hardware. Some were undoubtedly made locally by general blacksmiths, especially the large elaborate exterior examples which are rarely if ever found in Maine as original fixtures. Homemade wooden latches and bolts continued to be used on unimportant doors such as those to cellar, attic or outhouse. It is on these doors that the oldest hardware in the house is likely to be found.

MID-NINETEENTH CENTURY — 1900

By 1850 the machine-made "Blake's Patent Cast-iron Latch" was quickly replacing the handmade ones. This was used, mainly on less important doors, during the same period as the white ceramic door knobs. These knobs, with mortice locks, were usually fitted on the thicker (now mainly machine-made) doors. Sometimes they were fitted to a thin earlier door, either with a surface or box

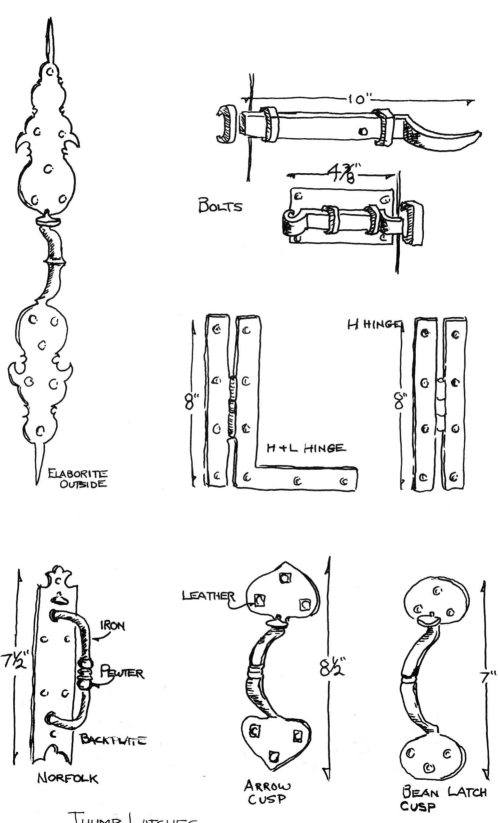

ELABORITE
OUTSIDE

10"

BOLTS

4⅞"

H HINGE

8"

H+L HINGE

8"

7½"

IRON

PEWTER

BACKPLATE

NORFOLK

THUMB LATCHES

LEATHER

8½"

ARROW
CUSP

7"

BEAN LATCH
CUSP

SUFFOLK LATCHES

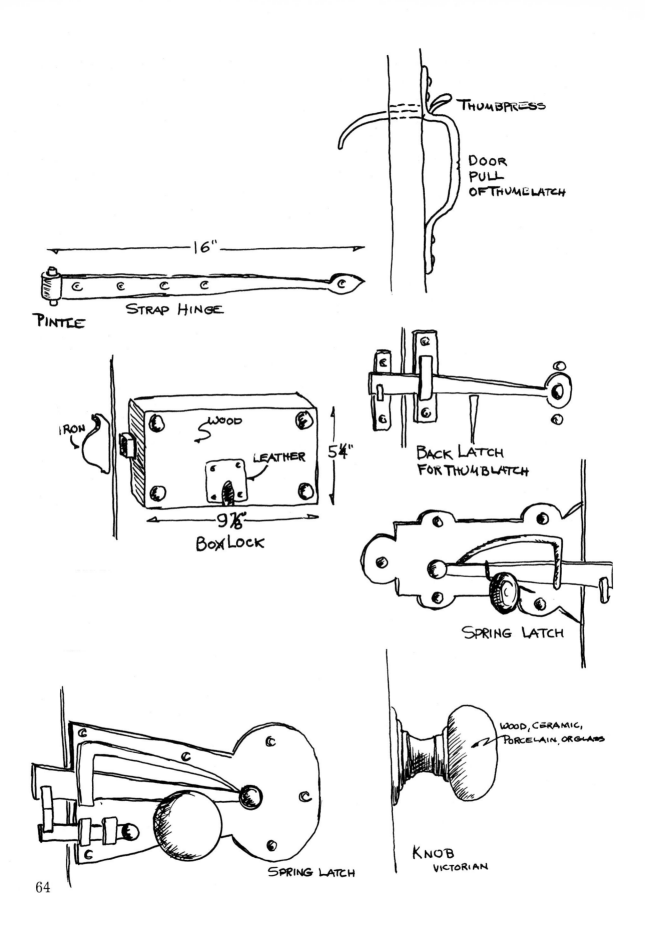

THUMBPRESS

DOOR
PULL
OF THUMBLATCH

16"

PINTLE

STRAP HINGE

IRON

WOOD

LEATHER

5¼"

9⅛"

BOX LOCK

BACK LATCH
FOR THUMBLATCH

SPRING LATCH

SPRING LATCH

WOOD, CERAMIC,
PORCELAIN, OR GLASS

KNOB
VICTORIAN

64

lock or a very thin mortice lock, to bring it up to date with changing fashions. The brown Bennington knobs appeared in the 1850's also and are found in Greek Revival and later in Victorian houses. The latter may also have the handsome silver mercury glass, black ceramic, walnut or stamped brass knobs. Painted porcelain knobs and finger plates, as well as milk and sandwich glass knobs, were popular. Elaborate sculptured brass fittings on windows and doors were also found. Stamped gilt curtain tiebacks and glass ornaments were much used.

Many handwrought hooks, catches, handles and bolts continued to be made to serve individual needs, although all these were readily available in manufacturers' catalogues by the 1860's in a machine-made form, often with elaborate embossed patterns on their surfaces to suit the taste of the time.

CLEANING OLD HARDWARE

Paint on loose hardware may be removed with paint remover, followed by cleaning with steel wool. Another good method is to immerse in tomato juice (a mild acid), cover, and simmer gently. Or try soaking in Coca Cola. After an hour or so scrub with water and steel wool. If more layers of paint remain repeat until it softens. This is also effective on brass. Finish by coating with linseed oil applied hot, or dull lacquer. If black paint must be used, add some red to it so that it is not so staring as flat black and will look more like old iron. Interior ironwork can be waxed and buffed to produce a satisfying mellow sheen. In many cases old hardware was painted to match its background and this is usually the best treatment if the original appearance of the room is desired. Some latch handles are trimmed with pewter which is soft and should not be scratched or heated.

REPLACING HARDWARE

Think carefully before removing later hardware that has been added to an earlier style room. For example, it may be preferable to keep a set of Greek Revival knobs that have been in the house for perhaps a hundred years rather than to substitute a poorly made inappropriate latch in the name of "restoration." If you do decide to go back to the original style of hardware, search carefully for clues in the paintwork of the door and its surround, and for evidence of earlier nail holes to determine the exact shape of the latch that was used. Good accurate reproductions are available and will give many years of satisfaction. Poorly scaled, stamped metal, modern replacements have nothing to recommend them.

The fine blacksmith-made latches are especially worthwhile for outside doors. A cylinder lock installed separately above the latch and painted the same color as the door will leave the emphasis on the handsome ironwork of the latch. However, if accuracy is desired, you will rarely find anything but a large scale Bean or Arrow cusp Suffolk Latch anywhere in Maine. Occasionally large Norfolk Latches were used.

Donald Streeter makes fine reproduction spring latches and bolts. Also see the catalogs of Horton, Vaughan, and Ball and Ball at the Greater Portland Landmarks Resource Center.

Strap hinges may be found in antique shops and easily installed; screw-in pintles to hang them on are available in some farm supply and hardware shops and are easier to install and adjust than the old driven pintles which are difficult to find. Most catalogs also carry strap hinges of varying qualities which come complete with pintle.

H and HL hinges in original pairs are very hard to find. Good reproductions are very expensive as they take a long time to make. (See Period Hardware, Ball & Ball, Vaughan, Donald Streeter) Adequate hinges made by Acorn are obtainable locally at L. C. Andrew, N. T. Fox, Freeport Country Store, and elsewhere. These can be improved by burning in the fireplace, then hammering or filing to make them a little less sharp and less smooth. This effect is similar to that produced (using the same basic steel hinge) by Leon Rockwell, Old Guilford Forge, and others. The shape and proportion is different from the old, as is the removable pin, but the hinges do not look too bad when painted to match their background, as was the usual custom.

In many cases it is better to settle for an unobstrusive butt hinge on the jamb edge of the door, especially where many hinges are needed.

Brass, and Ceramic Knobs (both white and brown) can still be found in antique shops for interior doors. There are small ceramic "apothecary" knobs from Old Guilford Forge and elsewhere in Country Stores. Or see Vaughan's Hardware Catalog.

Wooden Knobs and pulls for kitchen cabinets and drawers are obtainable from Shaker Workshops, Inc., Period Hardware and Horton Brass. L. C. Andrew and N. T. Fox will make them to your pattern in their cabinet shops in Portland.

Victorian Hardware - See Horton Brass, Period Hardware. Brass Hardware - O. P. Peterson, 384 Fore St., Portland, is a fine local source, or see catalogues as above.

There are no satisfactory latches available in local shops. These catalogs are available for reference at the Greater Portland Landmarks Resource Center. Actual examples of good reproduction latches are also on display there.

BLACKSMITHS

Donald Streeter
P.O. Box 237
Franklinville, New Jersey 08322

Richard W. Everett
The Salt Box
East Haddam, Connecticut 06423

Robert Bourdon
Greensboro, Vermont 05841

COMPANIES

Ball and Ball
"Whitford"
463 Lincoln Highway
Exton, Pennsylvania 19341

Period Furniture Hardware Co., Inc.
123 Charles Street
Boston, Massachusetts 01414

Horton Brass Co.
Box 95
Cromwell, Connecticut 06416

Leon Rockwell
Warehouse Point
Connecticut 06088

Old Guilford Forge
Guilford, Connecticut 06437

Old Smithy Shop
P.O. Box 226
Powers Street
Milford, New Hampshire 03055

Shaker Workshops, Inc.
Concord, Massachusetts 01742

W. C. Vaughan Hardware Co.
77 Washington Street, North
Boston, Massachusetts 02114

Williamsburg Blacksmiths, Inc.
Williamsburg, Massachusetts 01096
Note: This is not connected with Colonial Williamsburg.

REPLACEMENT HARDWARE AVAILABLE

NEW ENGLAND BLACKSMITHS MAKING HANDWROUGHT HARDWARE

The Strawbery Banke Blacksmith, Peter Happny, in Portsmouth, New Hampshire, will copy any hardware of which you can give him a pattern including delicate items such as latches and H hinges.

Williams Wasson of Freeport will make or copy fireplace or other heavy iron items. He does either forge or torch welding as requested.

Willis Reed of Yarmouth does torch welding and is good at mending things. He also makes fireplace cranes and rings if you take him a pattern.

The men listed above charge by the hour and do not use catalogs. Ask for an estimate of the cost.

Robert Bourdon, Greensboro, Vermont, will copy any pattern you send him, but also has a fine catalog of traditional hardware, based on the authoritative work of Albert Sonn. (See Bibliography of Building Hardware).

Richard Everett, East Haddam, Connecticut, does high quality work.

There are certainly others of whom we have no personal knowledge as yet. We would welcome details.

Donald Streeter of New Jersey is a master craftsman and probably the leading authority on traditional hardware in this country. His excellent catalog is a very good source of information.

Some smiths are producing accurate, beautifully made latches and other hardware in the same manner they were produced 200 years ago. These are a little more expensive than the partially stamped, reworked examples of Leon Rockwell, Old Guilford Forge, and others. And they cost considerably more than the dead black, flimsy, pressed metal latches ornamented with so-called "hammered" or "forged" edges made by Amrock, Acorn or Spencer so often seen on modern "Colonial houses." An inexpensive latch of good scale and weight is made by Williamsburg Blacksmiths, Williamsburg, Massachusetts. This has a good heavy back-latch which may be purchased separately for use with an antique pull. (Pulls are far easier to find in antique shops than a complete latch.)

67

BIBLIOGRAPHY

Old Sturbridge, Shelburne Museum and The Society For the Preservation of New England Antiquities have fine collections of hardware which repay study. Many museum houses still have their original hardware.

Dietz, Albert G. **Dwelling House Construction.** Princeton, N.J., Van Nostrand, 1946. Cambridge, Mass. M.I.T. Press, 1971.
  Available - GPL
    - PPL 690 D56
  'Hardware' Chapter 6, pp. 312-340. Description and uses of modern builders' finish hardware. Late Victorian to present day.

Kauffman, Henry J. **Early American Ironware, Cast and Wrought.** Rutland, Vermont, Tuttle, 1966.
  Available - PPL 739 qK21i
  The general working of iron, and manufacture of iron articles. Good chapter on locks and nails.

Kelly, J. Frederick **Early Domestic Architecture of Connecticut.** New Haven, Yale Univ. Press, 1924. New York, Dover reprint, 1963.
  Available - GPL Dover reprint
    - PPL 1924 ed. R728 qK29.
  Chapter 19, pp. 194-207. Good text...line drawings of early examples of wrought iron hardware.

Kettell, Russell Hawes, ed. **Early American Rooms: A Consideration of the Changes in Style...1650-1858.** Portland, Maine, Southworth Press, 1936. New York, Dover reprint, 1967.
  Available - GPL Dover reprint.
    - PPL 1936 ed. R747 qK43 Southworth
  Good architectural details (including hardware) and line drawings in rooms of different periods, through Victorian era.

Mercer, Henry C. **Dating of Old Houses.** Doylestown, Pa., Bucks County Historical Society, 1926.
  $1.00 (pamphlet 28 p.)
  Available - GPL
  Also reprinted in Old Time New England. Available PPL, R974 S67 Art, 1926, pp. 170-190. Early research on Pennsylvania examples. A work from which much later research has evolved.

Sonn, Albert H. **Early American Wrought Iron.** New York, Scribner's, 1928. 3v.
  Available - PPL R739 qS69
  The most comprehensive and beautifully illustrated work on the subject. (Three huge volumes). Many examples of all kinds of building hardware up to 1850's with their places of origin. New England examples included but in the minority.

Streeter, Donald **Early American Stocklocks.** (in Antiques, v. 98, August 1970, pp. 251-255)
  Available - PPL R050 A63 Art

Streeter, Donald **Early Wrought Iron Hardware: Spring Latches.** (in Antiques, v. 66, August 1954, pp. 125-127)
  Available - PPL R050 A63 Art

Watson, Aldren A. **Village Blacksmith.** New York, Crowell, 1968.
  Available - PPL 682 W33
  Excellent introduction to the working of iron. Well illustrated with clear pen sketches by the author.

Williams, H. L. **Old American Houses 1700-1850.** N.Y. Bonanza, 1957.
  Available - GPL
  pp. 101-109. Illustrated with good pencil sketches of hardware.

ARTICLES IN GPL RESOURCE CENTER

Donald Streeter has done several excellent scholarly articles on early wrought iron hardware and it is to be hoped that more will appear in future issues of the Bulletin of the Association of Preservation Technology.

His **Hardware Catalog** is also an excellent source of information, well illustrated with photographs.

Streeter, Donald **Hardware in Restoration.** (in Building Research, Sept.-Oct. 1964). Reprint of part of a panel discussion.

Streeter, Donald **Early American Wrought Iron Hardware: Norfolk Latches.** (in APT Bulletin, v. 3, no. 4, 1971).

Streeter, Donald **Early American Wrought Iron Hardware: H-HL Hinges, Dovetails, Cast Iron Butt Hinges** (in APT Bulletin v. V no. 1, 1973, pp. 22-49).

Streeter, Donald **Early American Wrought Iron Hardware: Some Signed American Rim Locks.** (in APT Bulletin, v. V no. 2, 1973, pp. 9-37).

Streeter, Donald **Early American Wrought Iron: English Iron Rim Locks.** (in APT Bulletin, v. VI no. 1, 1974, pp. 40-67).

Streeter, Donald **Early American Wrought Iron Hardware: Cross Garnet, Side and Dovetail Hinges.** (in APT Bulletin, v. VI no. 2, 1974, pp. 6-37).

INFORMATION ON NAILS

Bullock, Orin M., Jr. **Restoration Manual; an Illustrated Guide to the Preservation and Restoration of Old Buildings.** Norwalk, Conn., Silvermine Pubs., 1966.
Available - GPL

Mercer, Henry C. **The Dating of Old Houses.** Doylestown, Pa., Bucks County Historical Society 1926, $1.00.
Available - GPL

Nelson, Lee H. **Nail Chronology as an Aid to Dating Old Buildings.** American Association for State and Local History, 1315 Eighth Avenue South, Nashville, Tenn. 37203.
Technical Leaflet #48. (Appeared originally as a supplement to History News).
Available - GPL
Updates Mercer's Pioneer Work (see above).

Preiss, Peter **Wire Nails in North America.** (In APT Bulletin, v. V no. 4, 1973, pp. 87-92).
Available - GPL

Sloane, Eric **Museum of Early American Tools.** New York, W. Funk, 1964. Pp. 92-93.
Available - PPL 621.9 qS63.

Sloane, Eric **Reverence for Wood.** New York, W. Funk, 1965.
Available - PPL 620.12 qS63, p. 25

Smith, H. R. Bradley **Chronological Development of Nails.** Shelburne, Vermont. Shelburne Museum, Pamphlet #7.
Available - GPL

Wooden Latches and Bolts for batten doors may be made at home. We have several measured drawings of good original examples available for copying at the GPL Resource Center.

FABRICS AND WINDOW HANGINGS

There are many sources for historic fabrics and window hangings to guide the present home owner. Design books, diaries, inventories, prints, paintings, early periodicals as well as remaining original fabrics provide a wealth of information on textures, designs, varieties of material and use. In addition many modern companies are reproducing 18th and 19th century materials. The dates given here are only approximate and for local usage refer to the Architectural Style Text.

1700 - 1776: MATERIALS

By 1700 a variety of fabrics were available to the colonists. Many were spun and woven in the home, often in stripes, plaids or plan weaves. Sometimes the fabric was stitched or crewel embroidered in the Indian flower or tree-of-life motifs which were very popular in the 18th century. The colorful printed cottons or chintzes as well as various plain and patterned wools were imported by the colonists from England, France, India and through the China trade.

Satins, silks, brocades, and damasks were used for upholstery, window and bed hangings. In addition to these familiar fabric names, there were moreen: similar to today's moire, having a watered or cloudy appearance; china (cheyney): a worsted stuff; serge or camblet: a combination of wool, silk, and/or goat's hair fabric; calamenco: a glazed wooly fabric with narrow stripes or small checks; harrateen: a variety of linen. These were all used in the house as well as for clothing. Where possible these fabrics were used in strong colors of blue, yellow, green, and red. Yellow became most fashionable around the middle of the century, replacing the earlier popularity of green.

For upholstery, haircloth (horse or camel hair), leather, and Turkeywork were used as well as velvets, damasks, and satins. Wool still remained the stable textile, however, until the late 18th century when the British improved the spinning process and made cheap cotton possible.

In the North where commerce and trade flourished, many stately homes reflected current English taste by using the same fabric throughout a room. Research indicates, however, that window hangings were not often found throughout modest houses; often such a "luxury" was confined to the master bedroom, serving a decorative and useful heat retaining function. More typical at this time were the so-called "Indian Shutters", which were either of the sliding or folding variety. Often both types were seen in the same house.

1700 - 1776: WINDOW HANGING STYLES

Simple Curtains:

A single or double curtain hung to the sill or floor. Suspended from either cloth tapes or rings, it was gathered on a rod fitted into extending brackets, on a cord nailed within the frame, or simply tacked over the window. Occasionally the curtain was held back by a decorative cord, a tieback, or a handsome knob, and was closed as needed for warmth.

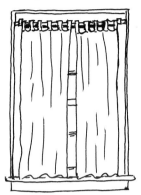

DOUBLE CURTAIN

SIMPLE GATHERED VALANCE

SINGLE CURTAIN

Valances:

For an informal room or house an extra piece of cloth, which was gathered to form a self-valance, added a decorative touch to many homespun curtains. For a more formal treatment a flat valance was hung from the frame, shaped at the lower edge and decorated with fringe or braid. Various styles were seen during the 18th century.

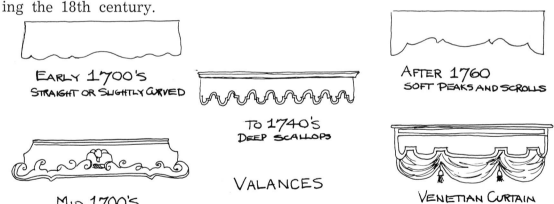

EARLY 1700'S
STRAIGHT OR SLIGHTLY CURVED

TO 1740'S
DEEP SCALLOPS

AFTER 1760
SOFT PEAKS AND SCROLLS

MID 1700'S

VALANCES

VENETIAN CURTAIN
WITH VALANCE

The Venetian Curtain:

This treatment, similar to today's Austrian or Viennese shades, consisted of cords run through a series of rings on the back side. Heavy coarse cottons, wool, or damasks were used, but a lighter weight would be more practical today.

Valances were also used with Venetian curtains. Often the lower edge of the curtain was fringed or tasseled to compliment the valance, especially when the curtains were drawn up.

1780 - 1815: FEDERAL MATERIALS

The classical feeling was sought during this period. This was due, in part, to the excavations at Pompeii. The Adams Brothers in England reintroduced many of these forms. Thomas Hepplewhite followed in the tradition and through his **Upholsterer's Guide** encouraged the use of stripes, ribbons, festoons, tassels, and shell and lotus patterns. Thomas Sheraton in his **Guide** suggested a lighter and more delicate feeling with urns, medallions and musical instruments on light silks, damasks and printed linen. Floral spray designs were especially popular and well suited to the softly draped curtains and delicate furniture of the time.

As the interior woodwork around the windows became more delicate so did the curtains. Materials were purchased in bolts and sometimes whole rooms were done in one fabric.

Cotton became more plentiful because of improved and developed copperplate and wood block printing techniques. Classical and pastoral scenes as well as patriotic heroes were reproduced. With these European printed cottons, Indian chintzes, embroidered mull (a sheer white cotton), pale silks, dimity and muslin complimented the more delicate furniture, china, and architectural styles of the period. Velvets, brocades and satins, when used, appeared in paler colors and more delicate prints than 18th century taste had demanded.

1780 - 1815: STYLES

Festooned Curtains:

This style replaced the heavy draw drapes. Like the Venetian curtains these were meant to be raised and lowered. When raised, the fabric was swagged at the top with cascades or jabots coming part way or all the way down to the sill. Evidence indicates that the curtain was made to pull to just one side as well as to both. Either way this effect is very decorative and is often created today.

FESTOONED CURTAIN
DRAWN TO ONE SIDE

FESTOONED CURTAIN

Valances:

Many variations of the valance were seen and are appropriate for today. Sometimes the curtain at the top was the only treatment used. Sometimes it was combined with long or short curtains.

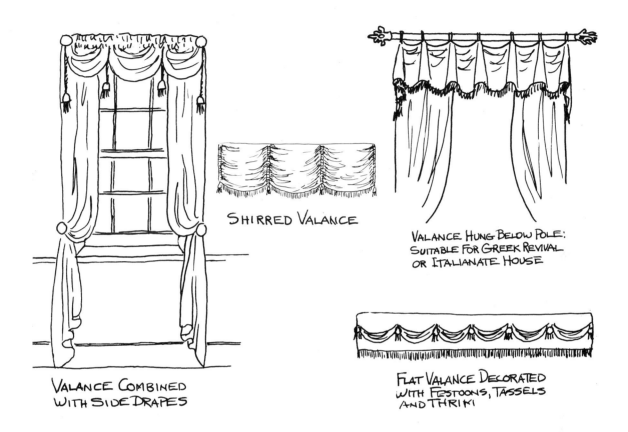

SHIRRED VALANCE

VALANCE HUNG BELOW POLE: SUITABLE FOR GREEK REVIVAL OR ITALIANATE HOUSE

VALANCE COMBINED WITH SIDE DRAPES

FLAT VALANCE DECORATED WITH FESTOONS, TASSELS AND THRIM

The French Curtain:

Thomas Sheraton in his **Drawing Book** (1793) gives us a description of the French curtains which were soon to become the "latest style" in hanging curtains. He writes "When the cords are drawn the curtains meet in the center at the same time, but are noway raised from the floor. When the same cord is drawn the reverse way, each curtain flies open and come to their place on each side."

Other Window Treatments:

Simple single or paired curtains, inside or outside the trim, hung to the sill, fringed and tied back, were often seen during the Federal period and are easily reproduced today.

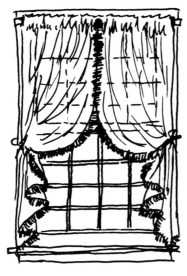

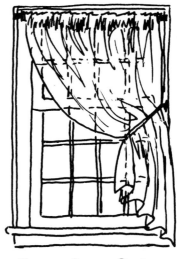

SIMPLE PAIRED CURTAINS

SINGLE CURTAIN DRAPED
TO ONE SIDE

Cornice Board:

A shallow wooden cornice board decorated with delicate mouldings or carved details, stenciled, painted or fabric-covered, often completed the window treatment.

Venetian Blinds:

Blinds made from thin lath and painted to match the woodwork were used alone or with curtains.

No Curtains:

Often no curtains were used, especially if the window had interior shutters or fine wood trim and carved plaster mouldings.

1815 - 1845   LATE FEDERAL OR EMPIRE MATERIALS

With the increased improvement in manufacturing textiles, the fabrics at this time continued to be plentiful and varied. Sheer white materials for curtains were seen. These included batiste, gauze, muslin, and mull, plain or dotted with embroidery and edged with white or colored ball fringe. These were often combined with heavier fabrics such as moreen, silk, satin, lampas (silk damask) or damask. Horsehair in plain and patterned weaves was used for upholstery. The design motifs were inspired from Greek vase paintings or the architectural decoration of ancient Rome. Thomas Jefferson's interest in Andrea Palladio's Roman Temple forms and the search for an official architecture for the new Republic, plus architects Latrobe and Town's popularization of the Greek forms, did much to bring about this last phase of the new classicism.

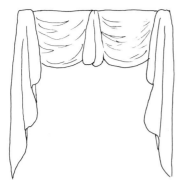

SIMILAR TO JEFFERSON'S
SKETCHES FOR MONTICELLO

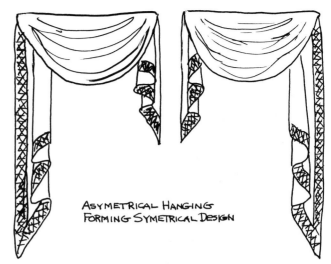

ASYMETRICAL HANGING
FORMING SYMETRICAL DESIGN

As the Period progressed, most of the earlier forms seen in the Federal Period gave way to heavier, less delicate, proportions. This happened not only in the furniture but also in the mouldings, trim, mantel and fireplace surrounds. Motifs such as bold acanthus scrolls and leafage, the anthemion and its accompanying fret and key designs, became more popular. The narrow stripe in material was replaced by a broader stripe in contrasting colors. Strong greens, deep blues, golden yellows were used. Marble appeared in darker tones and mahogany, with veneers of exotic woods, became fashionable. The emphasis in window draperies was in contrasting weight and color rather than textile pattern.

POLE WITH ELABORATE
TERMINALS

METAL TIE BACKS SHOW
RODS AND PULLIES CONCEALED

1815 - 1845 WINDOW HANGING STYLES

The French Curtain began to reflect the neoclassical and French Empire style of using long side drapes with sheer undercurtains. The side drapes were sometimes pulled to the side with metal tie backs. The exposed pole or rod was made of brass, iron or wood and made heavier with elaborate exposed ends.

Festoons:

The following variations of the festoon were often seen as the 19th century progressed: simple trimmed curtains of embroidered mull or batiste, suspended from a pole, draped aside on tie backs and all contained within the window moulding; a cornice over the valance; a curtain draped asymmetrically to form a symmetrical design. By around 1840 the fashion for venetian blinds was replaced by the use of lace curtains and window shades. These were made of transparent paper, canvas or cotton and painted with flowers or landscape designs. They often hung in the parlor or at staircase windows.

SWAG BEGINNING ABOVE THE POLE FROM CLASSICAL DESIGN

FRENCH DRAPES WITH POLE AND SWAG: SWAG COVERS MECHANISM

LIGHTLY DRAPED FABRIC OVER POLE w/CLASSICAL MOTIFS

1845 - VICTORIAN MATERIALS AND STYLES

During the Victorian Period the classic style was replaced by the romantic and sentimental revival. French and English baroque and rococo patterns were seen. Dark colors, crimson, maroon, deep blue, and bottle green became popular; and when combined with heavy fabrics such as worsted damask, lined silk, figured satins, brocatelle or merino cloth, gave a rich effect. Chintz was still used but was relegated to the bedroom. Berlin wool work (a worsted wool from merino sheep) was sought after for upholstery fabric, as well as silk plush and horsehair. Formal floral and stylized designs were fashionable and excessive fringe, tassels and fancy braid trimmings were used.

As the Victorian period progressed the window treatment became heavier. This was due in part to larger rooms and windows. It would not have been unusual to see in a formal parlor a window draped in layers of fabrics: a sheer curtain, a heavier draw curtain hung from rings on a heavy brass rod, with a heavier valance or "lambrequin" as it was called then, fringed and corded, falling half way or all the way to the floor and a brass, wood, gilt, or carved cornice over all.

Decorative shades continued to be used often in combination with other drapings.

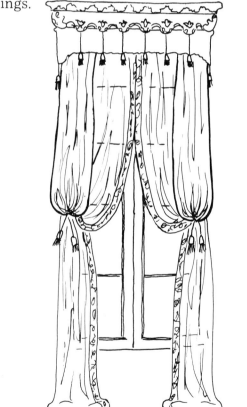

EARLY VICTORIAN PERIOD: CORNICE w/ VALANCE, SIDE DRAPES, AND SHEER CURTAINS

VALANCE WITH CORNICE WINDOW HANGING FOR A GOTHIC HOUSE

LATER VICTORIAN PERIOD: CORNICE, LAMBREQUIN, SIDE DRAPES AND SHEER CURTAINS

SOURCES

The following companies carry reproduction fabrics with authentic and appropriate designs suitable for an old house. These can be purchased through an interior designer. A few can be ordered through other outlets. By writing to the company at the common address of 420 Boylston St., Boston, Mass., you will learn where these fabrics can be ordered in your area.

The "*" indicates the companies which also carry companion wallpaper.

* Greeff Fabrics Inc.
* F. Schumacher
* Brunschwig and Fils
* Scalamandré Silks Inc.
  Strohein and Romann
  Arthur H. Lee & Sons
  Jofa Inc.
  Cyrus and Clark, Inc., 267 Fifth Ave., New York, N.Y. 10016

BIBLIOGRAPHY

Brightman, Anna **Woolen Window Curtains - Luxury in Colonial Boston and Salem.** (in Antiques, v. 86 no. 6, December 1964, pp. 722-727).
Available - GPL
   - PPL R050 A63 Art

Brightman, Anna **Window Curtains in Colonial Boston and Salem.** (in Antiques, v. 86 no. 2, August 1964, pp. 184-187).
Available - GPL
   - PPL R050 A63 Art

Brightman, Anna **Window Treatments for Historic Houses, 1700-1850.** Washington, D.C., National Trust for Historic Preservation, 1968. (Preservation Leaflet Series).
Available - GPL
Excellent source.

Clouzot, Henri **Painted and Printed Fabrics, the History of the Manufactory at Jouy and Other Ateliers in France 1760-1815. Notes on the History of Cotton Printing, Especially in England and America** by Frances Morris. New York, Metropolitan Museum of Art, 1927.
Available - PPL 745 qC64
Many lovely plates which show examples of painted and printed fabrics.

Connoisseur Period Guides to the Houses, Decoration, Furnishing and Chattels of the Classic Periods, ed. by Ralph Edwards and L. G. G. Ramsey. 6 vols. New York, Reynal, 1957-1958. 6 vols. in 1 New York, Bonanza, 1968.
   v.4 Late Georgian Period 1760-1810
   v. 5 Regency 1810-1830
   Available - PPL
            6v. edition 749 C75
            1v. edition 749 c75-b

Cummings, Abbott Lowell, comp. **Bed Hangings; a Treatise on Fabrics and Styles in the Curtaining of Beds, 1650-1850.** Boston, Society for the Preservation of New England Antiquities, 1961. 60 p.
Available - GPL

Fennelly, Catherine **Textiles in New England 1790-1840.** Meriden, Conn., Meriden Gravure Co., 1961. (Sturbridge Booklet Series).
Available - GPL

Flaherty, Carolyn **Drapes and Curtains.** (in The Old-House Journal, April 1974).
Available - GPL

Flaherty, Carolyn **Re-Creating Period Window Hanging.** (in The-Old-House Journal, May 1974).
Available - GPL
Very informative and helpful for those wishing to reproduce period window hangings.

Freeman, John C., Editor. **Furniture for the Victorian Home.** From A. J. Downing **Country Houses 1850,** J. C. Loudon **Encyclopedia** 1833, American Life Foundation 1968, N.Y. Watkins Glen Century House.
Available - PPL 749 F852

Hunter, George Leland **Decorative Textiles; an Illustrated Book on Coverings for Furniture, Walls and Floors, including Damasks, Brocades and Velvets, Tapestries, Laces, Embroideries, Chintzes, Cretonnes, Drapery and Furniture Trimmings, Wall Papers, Carpets and Rugs, Tooled and Illumined Leathers.** Phila., Lippincott, Grand Rapids, the Dean-Hicks Company, 1918.
Available - PPL R745 qH94

Keith, Graeme D. **Cotton printing.** (in Concise Encyclopedia of American Antiques. New York, Hawthorn, 1965).
Available - PPL R749 C73 Art

Lichten, Frances **Decorative Art of Victoria's Era.** New York Scribner, 1950.
Available - PPL R747 qL69

Little, Frances **Early American Textiles.** New York, Century Co., 1941.
Available - PPL 745 L77
An interesting account of the textiles made in this country from its beginning and into the machine age. Also information of the spinning and weaving and embroidery done in America.

Mailey, Jean **Printed Textiles in America.** (in Antiques, v. 69, no. 5, May 1956, pp. 422-427).
Available - GPL
      - PPL R050 A63 Art

Montgomery, Florence M. **Printed Textiles; English and American Cottons and Linens 1700-1850.** New York, Viking, 1970.
Available - GPL
      - PPL 746 qM787
A Winterthur Book. Many plates showing early textiles. Examples of bed and window hangings.

Pratt, Richard **Golden Treasury of Early American Houses.** New York, Hawthorn, 1967.
Available - GPL
Beautiful color photos of rooms from various restorations throughout the country.

Pray, M. **An Illustrated History of Furnishing from the Renaissance to 20th century.** George Braziller, N.Y. 1964.
Available - PPL R747 qP92
Many pictures of early paintings and prints which show interiors including many window hangings.

Preston, Paula Sampson **Printed Cottons at Old Sturbridge Village.** Meriden, Conn., Meriden Gravure Company, 1969. (Sturbridge Booklet Series) 37 p.
Available - GPL

Taylor, Lucy Davis **Story of Our Upholstery Fabrics: Characteristic Designs in Italy, France, and England from Early Times to the Seventeenth Century.** (in House Beautiful, v. 68, 356-8, October, 1930). **Of the Late Seventeenth and the Eighteenth Century.** (in House Beautiful, v. 68, pp. 478-480, Nov. 1930). **The Use of Old Fabrics in Rooms of Today.** (in House Beautiful, v. 68, pp. 620-644, 646-647, Dec. 1930).
Available - PPL

GARDENS

Plants and their disposition in the landscape, whether in their natural environment or in a man made garden, because of soil changes, growth, shift of position and hybridization, appear vastly different after a period of years. There is nothing stationary about a plant or an arrangement of plants; therefore, the gardens of the past cannot be measured and documented as can buildings.

Instead we will attempt to give here a brief resumé of the history of gardening in Europe and America, particularly as it influenced the gardens of New England.

During the last decades of the 17th century in England, landscaping was greatly inspired by the parks and gardens of Le Notre, the French designer of those at Versailles, where areas were arranged in geometrical patterns and the plants were pruned and prodded into formal designs.

Toward the end of the century, however, a movement developed which flourished throughout the Georgian period (1714-1837). Englishmen who had visited the continent returned home with an admiration for the work in landscape painting they had seen abroad, and their ambition was to reproduce the painted landscape in a natural setting.

In 1719 Lord Burlington induced a young Yorkshireman, William Kent, to return to England from Rome and complete the decorative painting at Burlington House in London. This painter and architect worked with Lord Burlington for the rest of his life, and contributed greatly to the development of English landscape design. He seems to have been the first to introduce a new kind of garden to England. Though he did not entirely discard the geometrical forms then in vogue, he substituted sunken fences ("ha-has") for the confining walls and through a less rigid arrangement allowed the garden to merge with the natural growth beyond.

Soon after Kent came Lancelot (Capability) Brown (1685-1748) who reduced the new irregular landscaping to a system of clumps, belts and lakes distributed in a closely mown greensward, which was cropped by sheep or cattle, as were the first great lawns of America. Ornamental buildings in the classical, Chinese, or Gothic style were distributed picturesquely.

The term picturesque as used in this earlier Georgian period implies a landscape reminiscent of the paintings of such artists as Claude Lorrain, Salvator Rosa and Gaspar Poussin.

A later picturesque period begins in 1794-5 with the publication of three books: **The Landscape, A Didactic Poem** by Richard Payne Knight (1750-1824); **Essay on the Picturesque** by Uvedale Price (1747-1829) and **Sketches and Hints**

80

on Landscape Gardening by Humphry Repton (1752-1818). There writers advocated a more natural treatment of the land than Capability Brown.

The developments in England, however, influenced only the layouts of large estates and of areas surrounding city mansions in America. The humbler citizens depended primarily upon what they or their forefathers had known at home; the seeds and plants which they could import, or cultivate from native stock; and the soil and climate of the land. Many plants were brought from England to America and by 1638 the apple, pear, plum, boxwood, European snowball, and English yew were well established here.

Innumerable lists of plants grown here are available for our study. In 1672 John Josselyn published in England a book entitled: **New England's Rarities Discovered,** and two years later he did a second volume, both giving descriptions of plants found in the new land. Through these volumes and other existing lists we know that the settlers grew foods necessary for sustenance such as fruits, vegetables and herbs, as well as flowers and imported shrubs.

In many phases of horticulture there was a time lag of nearly a century between developments in England and in America. For some two hundred years the settlers imported their best stocks from home, though many American plants traveled in the opposite direction and became established in English gardens.

As the quality of the colonists' lives improved the gardens reflected the change in status. Those of the affluent became more elaborate, following the English patterns of box and yew hedges, more formal arrangement of flower beds, and the introduction of topiary work and espaliered fruit trees. These last two practices were employed less in New England than in the south. The method of espaliering, however, was entirely practical in the north and recommended by Andrew Jackson Downing in his **Fruits and Fruit Trees of America,** for the cultivation of peach and other tender trees north of 43° latitude.

In the developing country, as more land was cultivated, the garden of the ordinary citizen expanded. Whereas originally flowers, herbs and vegetables were planted together, now often a kitchen garden existed for growing the vegetables and fruits needed for cooking, preserving and storing for winter and the housewife tended an enclosed flower garden growing plants for pure enjoyment. The New England garden of the countryman or villager has been likened to an English cottage garden of today.

From the beginning of the American settlement much nursery stock was imported from abroad, but the first commercial nursery was not opened until 1737. A botanic garden, though, had been established in Philadelphia by John Bartram in 1728. His house and grounds are now part of the Philadelphia park system. Bartram was widely consulted on matters of horticulture, and was visited in 1748-50 by Peter Kalm, a student of Linnaeus, the Swedish botanist, who upon Bartram's advice traveled through the northeast, collecting plants hardy in Swedish winters.

In 1737 a commercial nursery was established by Robert Prince at Flushing,

Long Island, New York. He not only imported seeds and plants from abroad, but he exported American plants to many parts of the world.

The selling of seeds in quantity began first in Philadelphia when David Landreth inaugurated a business that developed into a world trade in a few years. Soon after this time the Shaker sect from each of its settlements sold seed to all areas that could be reached by horse and wagon from the individual communities. Many of the gardens in the Portland, Maine, area must contain descendants of original Shaker plants from the Sabbath Day Lake farm.

We have previously mentioned the time lag in development in garden design between that of England and of America. This is most apparent in the acceptance of the picturesque style on this side of the Atlantic. It was promoted almost a half century later here, by the Hudson River aesthete, Andrew Jackson Downing, whose idols were, as had been those of the earlier landscapists, European painters, particularly in his case the Frenchman, Claude Lorrain, and the Italian, Salvator Rosa.

Downing advocated "a certain spirited irregularity" in landscape gardening with growth of "a somewhat wild and bold character". House styles he deemed suitable for such a background were: Gothic, the Early English, the Swiss Cottage (or cottage orneé), the Tuscan Villa, the Tudor Mansion, the Mansard Dwelling, and the one American contribution, the Hudson River Bracketed. Downing's work, **A Treatise on the Theory and Practice of Landscape Gardening Adapted to North America**, published in 1844, was the American bible of landscaping in its time.

This man, born in 1815, was drowned in the burning of the Hudson River steamer, Henry Clay, in 1852. His life was short, but his production immense, and had he lived longer he would undoubtedly have had even greater influence upon the development of landscaping in America.

Downing's contemporary, born only seven years later, seems much closer to our time, as he lived until 1903. We know of this man, Frederick Law Olmsted, as the designer of great parks, among them Central Park in New York and the Boston park system. We seldom, however, associate him with the landscaping of country houses in which specialty he also excelled. Among his New England achievements was the overall plan for the paths and roadways on Cushing's Island, in Casco Bay, Portland, Maine.

An associate of Olmsted was Calvert Vaux, who was born in London in 1824, met Downing in England in 1850, and formed a partnership with him which came to an untimely end with Downing's death in 1852. Vaux came to America at a time when architects were emigrating from England to participate in the building activity here and in Canada. English gardeners were also arriving to supervise or to work on the large estates, for horticulture had developed on a large scale.

During the 19th century many people had more leisure time, nurseries and seed firms were established, and transportation of goods was facilitated by the improvement of roads, the invention of the steamboat, and the building of canals and railroads.

The growing prosperity of the country also hastened the expansion of the interest in gardens. Wealthy men like William Coxe in New Jersey, Marshall P. Wilder in Massachusetts, and Nicholas Longworth in Cincinnati took leadership in fruit breeding, in importing ornamental shrubs and trees, and in developing exotic plants and new species in green houses. Under their leadership agricultural and horticultural societies and arboretums were established, and information on the best gardening practices became available to the general public through publications and garden displays as we know them today. A bibliography of available publications and a list of gardens open to the public in New England follow below.

HOUSES IN NEW ENGLAND
WITH GARDENS OPEN TO THE PUBLIC

This list includes gardens, either existing in much the same form as originally designed, or constructed from written description, general knowledge of the customs of the period, or conjecture. As has been stated, the character of the earliest New England gardens is largely conjectural. New knowledge is uncovered, new attitudes toward reconstruction develop, and gardens are planted, destroyed and replanted. The herb garden at Old Sturbridge Village, delightful to enjoy through charm of foliage, color and odor, is now considered wrongly conceived and in need of being replanted.

We offer this list of gardens for the pleasure of viewers of taste and discernment who will derive from them practical ideas for the enrichment of their own gardens.

MASSACHUSETTS

Boston

HEADQUARTERS HOUSE - 1807-08
Asher Benjamin, Architect
55 Beacon Street - open by appointment
National Society of Colonial Dames in the Commonwealth of Massachusetts.

NICHOLLS HOUSE MUSEUM - Early 19th Century
55 Mount Vernon Street - House designed by Charles Bulfinch - side entrance with dooryard garden enclosed by wrought iron railings - includes miniature brick patio, granite benches and flower beds.

Danvers	NURSE HOMESTEAD - 17th Century 149 Pine Street Situated on a knoll overlooking thirty acres of cultivated farmland.　　　　　　　　　SPNEA
	GLEN MAGNA - circa 1800 Route #1 - Paneling and details of house attributed to Samuel McIntire - summer house and gardens.
Gloucester	BEAUPORT Eastern Point Boulevard　　　　SPNEA
Hadley	FARM MUSEUM - barn built in 1782 Hadley Farm Museum Association
Ipswich	JOHN WHIPPLE HOUSE - 1640 A garden composed of 17th Century plants known to have been used by the original owners, their friends, and their neighbors, designed by Arthur A. Shurcliff, who was responsible for the Governor's Palace Garden at Williamsburg, and planted by Mrs. A. W. Smith, author of "Early American Gardens: 'for Meate or Medicine' ", (pen name Anne Leighton) see bibliography. The Ipswich Historical Society.
Lincoln	CODMAN HOUSE, "The Grange". 1735-41 Codman Road Imitation of an English Country Seat.　SPNEA
Marblehead	KING HOOPER MANSION - 1728 Headquarters of Marblehead Arts Association
Newburyport	CUSHING HOUSE 98 High Street - Newburyport Historical Society.
Norwell	JACOBS FARM - mid 18th Century Corner of Main Street and Jacobs Lane, Assinipi. SPNEA
Plymouth	PLIMOTH PLANTATION 126 Water Street Reconstructed Pilgrim village as of 1627. Gardens suggesting the period. Antiquarian House, formal garden.

84

Quincy	THE OLD HOUSE 135 Adams Street Built 1731 and enlarged several times, lived in by Adams family until 1927. Gardens complete as when occupied by Adamses. National Historic Site.
Rowley	PLATTS - BRADSTREET HOUSE - built 1670 183 Roxbury Street - English garden.
Salem	HOUSE OF THE SEVEN GABLES - 1668 54 Turner Street Gardens shown July and August PIONEERS' VILLAGE - Replica of village of 1630 with planting of the period. ROPES MEMORIAL - 1719 318 Essex Street - Formal gardens.
Stockbridge	MISSION HOUSE - 1739 Old fashioned garden.
Sturbridge	OLD STURBRIDGE VILLAGE Junction of Mass. Turnpike, Rts. 15 and 20 Farm garden and herb garden.
Waltham	LYMAN HOUSE - "The Vale" 1793 Lyman Street off Rt. 20 Grounds laid out in the manner of Humphry Repton by the Englishman, William Bell, believed to have been brought over for the work. The arched stone bridge over the brook, the pond, the greenhouses, summer houses and gardens are characteristic of the English work of the period. SPNEA
Waltham-Watertown	GORE PLACE - 1805 Extensive grounds laid out as of the period with stable and farm cottage.
Westfield	CHAUNCY ALLEN PARK Colonial herb garden

MAINE

Camden

SPITE HOUSE
Formal garden planted and maintained by the Camden Garden Club.
Open on House and Garden Day each year, the third Thursday in July.

Damariscotta

THE CHAPMAN-HALL HOUSE - 1754
The herb garden and rose border, planted and cared for by the Horticultural Committee of the Old Bristol Garden Club, consists of herbs used in colonial times and roses of the period.
Opposite the In-Town Damariscotta Information Bureau.

Portland

WADSWORTH-LONGFELLOW HOUSE - 1785
487 Congress Street
Green garden with brick edging and brick paths, with lilies, peonies, lilacs and hawthorn in season. Herb garden to be planted in 1975 - Maintained by the Longfellow Garden Club.

South Berwick

JEWETT MEMORIAL - 1774
Garden of traditional plants.
Route 236 - next to the public library   SPNEA

NEW HAMPSHIRE

New Ipswich

BARRETT HOUSE "Forest Hall" - 1800
Extensive grounds featuring an early garden house.
Main Street (off Route 124)   SPNEA

Portsmouth

THE LANGDON MANSION - 1784
143 Pleasant Street   SPNEA

MOFFATT-LADD HOUSE - 1763
Market Street
Terraced garden of the period.
The National Society of Colonial Dames in the State of New Hampshire.

86

RUNDLET-MAY HOUSE - 1807
364 Middle Street
Original courtyard and garden layout.   SPNEA

VERMONT

Brattleboro   "NAULAHKA" - home of Rudyard Kipling.
Perennial garden and wall garden (in the English tradition)

RHODE ISLAND

Newport   SANFORD-COVELL - 1869-70
72 Washington Street   SPNEA

North Kingston   CASEY FARM - 1750
Route 1A below bridge to Jamestown Island.
A working farm.   SPNEA

Wickford   SMITH'S CASTLE - 1677-78
A mile north on U.S. #1 at Cocumscussoc on site of a
trading post owned by Roger Williams. Restored garden.

CONNECTICUT

New Haven   PARDEE-MORRIS HOUSE - 1780
325 Lighthouse Road
Coach house and herb gardens.
New Haven Colony Historical Society.

Woodstock   HENRY C. BOWEN HOUSE
"Roseland Cottage" - 1846
Landscaped boxwood gardens and classical style garden
house.
Route 169 facing Woodstock Common.   SPNEA

BIBLIOGRAPHY

Bower, Frederick Orpen **Plants and Man, a Series of Essays Relating to the Botany of Ordinary Life.**
New York, MacMillan, 1925.
Available - PPL 581.6 B78

Brooklyn Botanic Garden **America's Garden Heritage** (pamphlet). Brooklyn, N.Y., 1968.
Available - GPL

Calkins, Carroll **Great Gardens of America.** New York, Coward McCann, 1969.
Available - GPL

Carmer, Carl **The Hudson.** New York, Farrar and Rinehart, 1939.
Available - PPL 974.7 C28h
Contains an interesting chapter on the life and accomplishments of A. J. Downing.

Cobbett, William **A Years Residence in the United States.** London, Sherwood, Neely and Jones, 1816.
Available - PPL W973.54 C65

Downing, Andrew Jackson **A Treatise on the Theory and Practice of Landscape Gardening** - 1841 posthumously published New York, C. M. Saxton Co. 1857, New York, Orange Judd 1875, reprint New York, Funk and Wagnalls 1967.
Available - PPL 710 D75

Earle, Alice Morse **Old Time Gardens.** New York, Macmillan Co., 1928.
Available - PPL 716 E12
Rather fanciful and sentimental in style, yet seemingly well researched and worth reading; particularly for its descriptions of New England gardens. No bibliography, one must search through for sources of information.

Fairbrother, Nan **Men and Gardens** (History of Gardening). New York, Knopf, 1956.
Available - PPL 716 F15
Scholarly and literary. She omits the 19th century which she considers insignificant in garden history.

Favretti, Rudy F. **Early New England Gardens, 1620 - 1840.** Sturbridge, Mass. Old Sturbridge Village, 1962 - 1966.
Available - GPL
Brief resume of the history of gardens in New England with illustrations from Old Sturbridge Village.

Favretti, Rudy F. and DeWolf, Gordon P. **Colonial Gardens** Barre, Mass., Barre Publishers, 1972.
Available - GPL
Description of plants cultivated by early American colonists, with alphabetical lists, and illustrations from old herbals.

Hill, Thomas **First Garden Book; Being a Faithful Reprint of a Most Briefe and Pleasaunt Treatyse, Teaching Howe to Dress, Sowe and Set a Garden, by Thomas Hyll, Londyner, 1563.** Collated and edited by Violet and Hal W. Trovillion. Herrin, Ill., Trovillion Private Press, 1938.
Available - PPL 635.7 H64

Howells, John Mead **The Architectural Heritage of the Merrimack.** New York, Architectural Book Publishing Co., Inc. 1941.
Available - PPL R728 qH85m

Howells, John Mead **The Architectural Heritage of the Piscataqua.** New York, Architectural Book Publishing Co., Inc. First published 1937, reissued 1965.
Available - GPL
- PPL R728 qH85
Photographs of and comments on buildings and interiors of the Portsmouth, N.H. area from 17th century through the Greek Revival period. An excellent record of past architectural achievement and of garden plans, as many of the buildings have been altered, moved or razed, and the gardens destroyed since the photographs were taken.

Jekyll, Gertrude **A Gardener's Testament.** New York, C. Scribner's Sons 1937.
Available - PPL 716 J47gt

Josselyn, John **An Account of Two Voyages to New England Made During the Years 1638 - 1663 by John Josselyn, gent.** Boston, W. Veazie, 1865.
Available - PPL R974 J84

Kalm, Peter (Pehr) **Travels Into North America** translated by John Reinhold Foster. Barre, Mass., Imprint Society, 1972.
Available - PPL R917.3 K14

Leighton, Ann **Early American Gardens.** Boston, Houghton Mifflin Company, 1970.
Available - PPL 635 L52
A description of Puritan gardens in 17th Century New England, with emphasis upon their practicality and simplicity, likening them to present day English cottage gardens.

Phipps, Frances **Colonial Kitchens, Their Furnishings and Their Gardens.** New York, Hawthorn, 1972.
Available - GPL

Robinson, William **The English Flower Garden** (Victorian). First published in 1883. London, J. Murray 1901. New York, Scribner's, 1926.
Available - PPL 716 R66
Design and arrangement of gardens in Great Britain and Ireland.

Schmitt, Carl F. **Fences, Gates and Garden Houses.** Rochester, N.Y., Carl F. Schmitt, 1963.
Available - GPL
Photographs and measured drawings of styles of various periods.

Simmons, Adelma Grenier **Herb Gardening in Five Seasons.** New York, Hawthorn Books, Inc., 1964.
Available - GPL
The history, description and culture of a variety of herbs, with recipes for use, line drawings, garden plans and photographs.

Stewart, John J. **Historic Landscapes and Gardens.** Technical Leaflet #80. American Association for State and Local History News. Vol. 29, No. 11, November 1974. A.A.S.L.H., 1315 Eighth Avenue, South, Nashville, Tenn. 37203.
Available - GPL

Summerson, John **Architecture in Britain 1530 - 1830.** London, Penguin Books Ltd., 1953. Revised and rearranged edition 1955.
Available - PPL 720.942 qS95
Concise and illuminating accounts of gardens and landscaping in England during this period.

VonMiklos, Josephine **Good Fences Make Good Neighbors.** New York, Charles Scribner's Sons, 1972.
Available - GPL
Photographs of walls and fences in America with brief descriptions.

White, Katharine S. **Onward and Upward in the Garden.** 11 Xeroxed articles from the New Yorker - March 1, 1958 (missing); March 14, 1959; September 26, 1959; March 5, 1960; September 24, 1960; March 11, 1961; June 9, 1962; December 18, 1965; December 10, 1966; November 4, 1967; November 11, 1967; December 16, 1967. New York, The New Yorker magazine.
Available - PPL 716 qW58
Delightful accounts of gardening in Blue Hill, Maine, with much valuable advice and information on sources for seeds, plants and cultivation, and guides to garden literature.

Winthrop, John **History of New England** 1630 - 1640. Winthrop's Journal, edited by James Kendall Hosmer New York, C. Scribner's Sons, 1908.
Available - PPL 974.4 W79
A day by day recording of the voyage to, and life in the Massachusetts Bay Colony.

Winthrop, Robert Charles **Life and Letters of John Winthrop.** Boston, Ticknor and Fields 1864-67.
Available - PPL B W792w

Wood, William **New England's Prospect.** Reprint of original edition. Printed at London by the Cotes, for Jolm Bellamie 1934. Boston, Prince Society 1865.
Available - PPL W973 W88
"A true, lively and experimental description of that part of America commonly called New England; discovering the state of that Countrie, both as it stands to our newcome English planters; and to the old native inhabitants."

SOME GUIDELINES
FOR MOVING OLD HOUSES

"The method to be employed in moving any antique house will depend upon a great deal more than the whim of the owner. The size and shape of the house, its construction, the terrain to be transversed, the obstacles to be encountered, the distance, and above all the cost of permissions, all need to be considered. Moving any house is a minor miracle of engineering and moving an antique house whether of wood or masonry calls not only for skill and experience but for understanding and a feeling for the old structure and what it represents to the owner." So say the Williams in their book **Old American Houses** on page 166.

Whether your house will be moved in one piece, cut or dismantled, will have to be a decision made by the mover after assessing the job to be done. If the house has its chimney or chimneys intact, inquire about the possibility of moving them as well. This has been done successfully in many cases, and since the original fireplaces add a great deal to the charm of these early houses, it is well worth the extra effort. If moving the chimney is not feasible, be sure to photograph and measure chimney and fireplace openings carefully to aid in accurate restoration.

It is important to judge the house by the number and quality of early features and not to be deterred by dirt or modern cover-ups (wallboard over paneling, linoleum covered floors, etc.). Checking your house for soundness before the move is essential. Sills should be suspect, and carefully inspected by removing the bottom clapboards. The extent of rot is not always obvious from the inside. (See: "On Preservation, Restoration, Renovation, And Care" in this folder).

Once you have made the decision to move an early house, there is much you must do to insure its successful completion.

The listing that follows has been compiled by "Fellow House Movers" in the hope that these steps will help make your move progress more smoothly.

LAND ACQUISITION
1. Make sure the land is adequate to accept the house.
2. To avoid disappointment, check local zoning ordinances to see if they allow for intended use.

PERMITS AND WIRES
1. Some movers take care of all necessary moving permits; others expect you to do this. Inquire.
2. Check with town officials, utilities (telephone and power) and railroads, if

necessary. Expect and plan for delays.

3. Local permits covering excavation, foundation, etc. are your responsibility. Allow plenty of time for delays and red tape, human nature being what it is.

2 STORY, 1 ROOM DEEP, COLONIAL HOUSE;
MOVED FROM PORTLAND TO FALMOUTH.

EXCAVATION AND FOUNDATION

1. Occasionally the mover has his own men to do this preliminary work and will be responsible for results. More frequently, however, this will be your job (or that of your contractor). Remember that old houses are rarely square, so measure with a transit to make sure the new foundation will fit the house.

2. Plan ahead for use of original foundation stones or providing a lip on the new, poured foundation to accept a brick facing.

MASON
1. Try to choose a mason who is knowledgeable regarding early techniques, or one who is willing to learn, so that the fireplaces and chimney will look as much like the originals as possible. If only repairs are necessary, the method is still important. Technique used on hidden areas can be a matter of individual judgment.
2. If you hope to move the internal chimney intact, have it checked by your mason first to make sure it is feasible.
3. Remember to save and mark the face bricks individually, and take careful measurements and photographs of fireplaces and chimney before dismantling if they are to be rebuilt. (See: "Fireplaces and Chimneys" in this folder).

SEWER OR SEPTIC

WATER
Town or well.

ELECTRICITY AND TELEPHONE
1. Outside - these should be underground, if possible. If the power company tries to discourage you - be persistent. It can be done.
2. Inside - try to have the electrical outlets and telephone jacks conveniently located and inconspicuous. Make decisions ahead regarding their placement and then supervise the actual installation.

PLUMBING
Hiding the pipes or placing them so as to be the least noticeable is well worth the extra effort required. Do not allow cutting or boring of structural timbers, as this weakens them.

CARPENTRY
1. It is extremely important to find a craftsman who is either well versed in early construction or one who has an appreciation of same.
2. If the house is cut, the carpentry work necessary to put it back together will not be part of the mover's services.

VANDALISM
Unfortunately, uninhabited houses are prime targets. Bricks, doors, hardware, floor boards, etc. may all disappear overnight.

The responsibility for coordinating the above aspects of the move and subsequent restoration is of the utmost importance and must be assigned to a competent person (either yourself or a reliable contractor). It is also important that the workmen be chosen with care, and then supervised.

2½ STORY, SQUARE, EARLY FEDERAL PERIOD HOUSE; MOVED FROM WEST CUMBERLAND TO CUMBERLAND FORESIDE.

Something you might not think to consider when planning your move is the time of year. But, in our climate, this can have a direct bearing on the ease with which it is accomplished.

Once again we would like to remind you of the importance of thinking carefully before making any irreversible changes or throwing anything away. If in the final analysis you choose to make changes, record the house as it was originally, with photographs. (See: "Keeping Restoration Records" in this book)

If, after you have made your plans, and enthusiastically presented your proposals to the bank, you get negative results, don't be discouraged. Persevere—try another bank.

Along these lines it may be encouraging to know that there is insurance available to cover your house while enroute. We understand that some policies will even cover the chimney if that is being moved. Do inquire.

Probably no one who has not been through the total involvement which moving an old house requires can fully appreciate the immense satisfaction, pleasure and continuing pride which the experience of saving and restoring an old house can bring. Let those who have done it speak for themselves.

"It went together like a piece of cake"

"I would do it again"

"A rewarding experience"

"It is satisfying to know that an old house has been saved from demolition to be used and enjoyed by generations to come"

"Your house looks as though it had always been there"

If in your own experience you discover additional tips that would be helpful to others embarking on a similar adventure, GPL would like to hear from you.

BIBLIOGRAPHY

Williams, Henry Lionel and Ottalie K. **Old American Houses, 1700-1850. How to Restore, Remodel and Reproduce Them.** N.Y. Bonanza, 1957.
Available - GPL

94

FINANCING RESTORATION WORK
ON OLD HOUSES

In general, financing restoration work on an old house through a local bank, credit union or other lending institution is not too different from financing a new house. The lender will be concerned with the same issues of your credit rating, the location of the property, its appraised value, and the demonstrated feasibility of the work which you propose.

In dealing with a lender, the key point to remember is to do your homework and know the costs and values associated with your proposal. As most bank appraisers value property based upon similar properties recently sold in the local market, as well as potential income and replacement costs, it is wise to have some knowledge of other "historic" homes which have been bought recently. It is also helpful to prepare a "pro forma" operating statement showing the anticipated costs and incomes from the property and a "pro forma" capital budget showing the cost of the property and its restoration and the proposed sources of the money, including the requested loan. Your local library will be able to provide you with books showing how these statements are easily prepared.

Remember, in the case of small single family or duplex owner-occupied buildings, banks will generally be willing to accept a higher per dwelling unit cost because they will take into account your own credit standing and your willingness to pay a higher than average monthly price for the type of housing you desire. However, if the property is a multi-family building, the lender will want to be assured that the income from this property covers all costs and provides for a small surplus.

Be sure to have a detailed estimate of the time and money necessary to complete the restoration work which you propose. Most banks are wary of restoration projects because many tend to drag on for years and run over initial cost figures. Have several reliable and experienced contractors' estimates available for the bank's information. And don't be afraid to discuss the estimates with the contractors. Many times a contractor will be able to save you money by suggesting an alternate approach to a problem. Saving money improves your chances of having a lender say yes to your proposal.

Often, you may be eligible for some type of government program to assist you in purchase or restoration of the older house. In addition to the "FHA" and "VA" mortgage programs, there are several U. S. Department of Housing and Urban

Development programs to insure "home improvement" loans. If your house is within certain locally designated urban renewal or neighborhood development areas, you may be eligible for low-interest loans. Call your town or city hall and ask if any such programs exist. Although you may not be in an eligible area, if your local government is running such a program you may possibly convince your city council to extend it into your area in the next budget year.

If your house is listed on the National Register of Historic Places or is in a National Register Historic District, you are eligible to apply for a matching grant from the Department of the Interior. These grants provide up to half of the cost of work necessary to stabilize a property in danger of destruction due to neglect or other action, and for work on the exterior and other areas visible to the general public. At present this program has little money and most projects approved have been for significant public buildings. Still, you may make application by writing to the State Historic Preservation Officer in your state capital.

Finally, do not hesitate to be frank and open with your banker. If you have been doing business with a particular bank for any period of time, speak with the manager of the branch where you do business and explain to him what you want to do. Ask for his suggestions and comments on your proposal. It is entirely proper to ask him on what criteria his bank and other banks in your area evaluate loan applications for restoration projects. Design your proposal to meet these criteria.

If all else fails, you may consider borrowing against other collateral such as other property, savings, stocks, or securities. This may give you the money necessary to do a substantial portion of what you wish and, although it is a less desirable approach, you may then go to local lenders, having demonstrated the feasibility of the project. Many times lenders will be willing to reconsider a substantially completed project because the risks and uncertainties of visualizing proposed work are eliminated.

Remember, although a restored historic house may seem ideal to you, your banker is concerned that you may not be able to find someone else to share your dream when and if you try to sell your house. For this reason avoid anything which may strike your banker as too "flippy" or "avante-garde" based upon contemporary housing standards.

Properly planned and presented, the historic house restoration can be a workable and bankable project.

HISTORIC HOUSES IN MAINE
OPEN TO THE PUBLIC

Dates, times and admission fees can vary, so it is wise to check before traveling to visit a site. Unless otherwise mentioned, all buildings listed are open to the public at certain times.

LADY PEPPERRELL HOUSE, 1760
Kittery Point
On Route 102, four miles east of Portsmouth, N.H.

An elaborate late Georgian mansion with hip roof, projecting pavilion facade, quoining. Contains great fireplaces, fine woodwork and fine period furniture. SPNEA.

JEWETT MEMORIAL, 1774
South Berwick
On Route 236, in center of town

Birthplace and home of authoress Sarah Orne Jewett. A mid-Georgian frame house with hip roof, dormer windows, four chimneys and portico. Contains decorative hand-carved woodwork, Georgian center staircase. Rooms have early wallpapers, carpets and antique furnishings of various periods. Outside are good examples of brick walk and garden. SPNEA.

HAMILTON HOUSE, 1785
South Berwick
Vaughan's Lane. Turn left off Route 236 opposite Junction with Route 91.

Fine Georgian country house of a ship builder and trader, overlooking river in beautiful setting with elaborate garden. Contains lovely Georgian and Federal furniture and hall wallpaper duplicated from the original. Authentic colors of paint used, based on scrapings. An earlier small house has been moved into the garden. SPNEA.

ELIZABETH PERKINS HOUSE,
c1732 (with 1686 wing)
York
On South Side Road at Sewall's
Bridge on the York River

A two-story center chimney frame house attached to a small 17th century dwelling. Both parts have sliding interior shutters. Contains a "good morning" stairway, an area on the second floor where room occupants on either side might meet on the way to breakfast. Furnished with antiques of various periods, including many of Victorian vintage.

WILCOX HOUSE, 1740
York
On Route 1A near center of town

House with a varied past—enlarged in 1756 and 1819 with alterations through the years, when it served as private home, tavern and post office. Parlor and bedchamber above have simple Federal mantelpieces and paneling. The older kitchen has vertical and horizontal sheathing. Mulberry tiles frame parlor fireplace. Has a walk-through chimney passage and a taproom restored as when used for a stagecoach stop.

JEFFERDS TAVERN, c1760
York
York Street, just off Main Street

A red clapboard two-story salt box, moved from Wells where it was a refreshment stop on the Kings Highway. Restored taproom has bar adapted from Wayside Inn (South Sudbury, Mass.) design. Interesting vertical panels above kitchen fireplace.

OLD GAOL MUSEUM, 1720
York
Main Street, opposite post office,
Route 1

The oldest existing English public building in America, part has early stone construction, part frame with gambrel roof. Jail in use till 1860. Jailer's living quarters contain furnishings of the period, including unique crewelwork bed hangings done more than 200 years ago. Also houses collections of early lighting devices, cooking equipment and china.

WILLOWBROOK
Newfield
Route 11

A recently assembled museum village of the Victorian era. Includes two homesteads decorated and furnished in the period, schoolhouse replica and large barn housing collection of sleighs and buggies, plus displays of such trades as blacksmithing, harness-making, laundering.

DANIEL MARRETT HOUSE,
1789
Standish
Route 25, center of town

Center-chimney Georgian house remodeled in Greek Revival style. Has good Greek Revival kitchen fireplace, fine door hardware. Contains family portraits and furnishings of Federal and Empire styles. SPNEA.

HAWTHORNE HOUSE, early
19th century, 1839
South Casco

Two and one half-story ten-room frame house built by an uncle of Nathaniel Hawthorne, who lived there as a boy from 1813 to 1825. In 1839 the house was remodeled as a meeting house. Owned by the South Casco Historical Society.

PARSON SMITH HOMESTEAD,
1764
South Windham
89 River Road, approximately
3 miles north of the center
of Westbrook

High-style early two and one-half story frame house, partially remodeled in early 19th century. Contains Georgian paneling and several folding partitions, a good Federal mantel in the front parlor, interesting kitchen fireplace, good hardware. Open by appointment. SPNEA.

BAXTER MUSEUM, c1800
Gorham
63 South Street

Two and one-half story Federal house with dormers. Part of the South Street Historic District, home of the Baxter family which produced the historian-philanthropist, James P. Baxter, and his son, Gov. Percival P. Baxter, one of the state's great benefactors. Contains relics of Gorham history. Belongs to the town.

TATE HOUSE, 1755
Portland
1279 Westbrook Street
Stroudwater, near airport

A three-story clapboard house with unusual gambrel roof, running dormer and large center chimney. Contains fine paneling, bolection moulding in dining room, cove ceiling in hall, 18th century furniture. Good example of diamond-painted floor in hall. Owned and maintained by the National Society of Colonial Dames of America in Maine.

NEAL DOW HOUSE, 1829
Portland
714 Congress Street, Downtown

The home of Gen. Neal Dow, leading 19th century proponent of prohibition, mayor of Portland and candidate for U.S. presidency on the Prohibition ticket. A late Federal style house of brick with Greek Revival and Victorian details, including tin ceilings and interesting lighting devices. Owned by the Womens' Christian Temperance Union.

WADSWORTH-LONGFELLOW HOUSE, 1785
Portland
487 Congress Street, Downtown

The first brick house in Portland. Raised from two to three stories in 1815. Was boyhood home of Henry Wadsworth Longfellow and contains various possessions of the Wadsworth and Longfellow families. Garden. Owned by the Maine Historical Society.

McLELLAN-SWEAT HOUSE, 1800
Portland
103 Spring Street, Downtown
Enter through Museum of
Art on High Street

A three-story Federal mansion designed and built by Portland housewrights, John Kimball, Jr. and Sr. Has Palladian windows, elaborate doorway, flying staircase. Contains many documented McLellan portraits, silver pieces and furnishings, as well as other Colonial and Federal furniture. Also houses large collection of mid 19th-century Portland glass. Maintained by Portland Society of Art.

VICTORIA MANSION, 1859
Portland
Park and Danforth Streets,
Downtown

Considered the finest example of a Victorian Italian villa in the French style in this country. Also called the Morse-Libby House, it is a two-story brownstone dwelling with three-story tower. Features frescoed walls and ceilings, hand-carved marble fireplaces, flying staircase with hand-carved mahogany balusters, and many original furnishings. Owned and maintained by the Victoria Society of Maine Women.

SHAKER VILLAGE
Poland Spring
Route 26, near
Sabbathday Lake

The 1794 meetinghouse is a very unusual example of early meeting house, but typical of Shaker architecture elsewhere. It is a two and one-half story gambrel-roofed building with a remarkable open floor plan for such an early building. It and the elders' house, which is also open to the public, have original interior paint. Museum buildings contain exhibits of Shaker furniture, tin, woodenware, tools, textiles. Not just a museum, but one of the two still active Shaker communities.

HOLMES-CRAFTS HOMESTEAD, c1820
North Jay

A well-preserved Federal style house.

HISTORY HOUSE, 1839
Skowhegan

Well-preserved one and one-half story brick house of Greek Revival style. Contains artifacts illustrating Skowhegan history.

BLAINE HOUSE, 1830
Augusta
The Governor's Mansion
192 State Street

House complex is composed of two hip-roofed blocks, each with Italianate cupola, connected by a two-story ell. Has undergone at least two remodelings. Was purchased by James Blaine, presidential candidate, in 1862. Donated to the state in 1919 and remodeled then by John Calvin Stevens with neo-colonial touches added. Contains twenty-eight rooms with nine fireplaces. Part of first floor open to the public.

FORT WESTERN, 1754
Augusta
Bowman Street, along east side of Kennebec River

Original fort of twenty rooms built by the Plymouth Company for defense and storage during the French and Indian Wars. Trading post, soldiers' kitchen and barracks, and officers' quarters have been restored and furnished with 18th and early 19th century pieces. Several rooms have wainscoting. Also houses exhibits of historic interest, military articles, Indian items and a room devoted to spinning and weaving.

POWNALBOROUGH COURT HOUSE, 1761
Dresden
On Route 128, 2.7 miles southwest of Maine Turnpike, Exit 14

Remarkable for its large size, commanding river position and early construction methods, this three-story hip roof house is 45 feet long and 44 feet wide. In addition to housing the county court from 1761-1794, it also served as Plymouth Company offices, meeting house, dwelling, tavern and post office. Interior features include many large fireplaces and some vertical plank walls. Contains a comprehensive exhibit including scale models illustrating the ice industry on the Kennebec.

NICKELS-SORTWELL HOUSE, 1807
Wiscasset
Corner of Main & Federal
Streets — Route 1

A high-style three-story Federal mansion, featuring a Palladian window and leaded glass semi-circular window on third floor. Has a columned portico, elliptical hall, flying staircase and ornate carving around doors and windows. The hand-carved parlor fireplace has free-standing columns. SPNEA.

LINCOLN COUNTY JAIL
1809 and 1837
Wiscasset
Turn left off Route 1 on
Federal Street in center of
town, follow signs

Jail of dressed granite built in 1809 as principal prison for Maine. Attached brick Greek Revival jailer's house built in 1837 with four end chimneys. House now used as Museum of Maine Arts and Crafts. Owned by the Lincoln County Cultural and Historical Assn.

CHAPMAN-HALL HOUSE, 1754
Damariscotta
on Business Route 1, opposite
town information bureau

A typical cape-style farmhouse of the Colonial period. Interesting paneling, wainscoting of two different periods and authentic furnishings of 1754-1820 era. Original floors. Has example of interior vertical plank wall. Herb garden and rose border.

MONTPELIER
Thomaston
On Route 1, 12 miles
east of town center

A 1929 reproduction of the 1795 General Henry Knox Mansion which was taken down in 1871 when the railroad went through. A majestic two-story structure with matched board facade, eighteen rooms. Interior details include a flying staircase, an oval room and furnishings of the period.

FARNSWORTH HOMESTEAD, 1840
Rockland
Elm Street, behind Farnsworth
Museum

A Greek Revival mansion of eleven rooms with Victorian decor and furniture.

CONWAY HOUSE, 18th century
Camden
Route 1 and Conway Road

A cape-style center chimney farmhouse. Interior shows three periods in the house's history, with floor and window treatments done accordingly. Buttermilk paints created to match original colors. An unusual curved entrance hall has a "parson's cupboard." Large heavy-timbered barn has collection of carriages and early tools. Plantings on grounds are all of plants in use in New England before 1860.

JOHN PERKINS HOUSE,
1765, 1783
Castine

Castine's only pre-Revolutionary dwelling. It survived the British bombardment of 1779 and enemy occupation in the War of 1812. Recently dismantled and moved to present location. A good example of Vernacular Georgian architecture. Includes hearse house and blacksmith shop.

PARSON FISHER HOUSE, 1814
Blue Hill
Main Street, 1 mile out of town
at intersection of Routes
176 and 172

A unique two-story hip-roofed frame house designed and built by Rev. Jonathan Fisher, first minister of the town, who was also a writer, painter, inventor and missionary. Good hardware, especially door latches. Full of Fisher's creations.

HOLT HOUSE, 1815
Blue Hill

A square hip-roofed Federal style village house, home of the Blue Hill Historical Society. Fireplaces in each of its eight rooms. Delicate rope carving around windows and doors. Handsome fence and rosette gate are copies of the originals.

BLACK MANSION, 1824-1827
Ellsworth
On Route 172, West Main Street

A two-story brick mansion of Federal design with colonnaded one-story porch across main front. Balustrades on porch, main house and wings. Contains graceful spiral staircase. Built as home and office of land agent following a plan of Asher Benjamin. Remains as furnished and used by three generations of the Black Family. The landscaped grounds contain a carriage house with collection of carriages and sleighs.

SONOGEE, 1903
Bar Harbor
North of ferry terminal
on Route 3

A forty-room mansion on six formal acres, modeled after an Italian villa. Once owned by Vanderbilts, it is one of the few Bar Harbor millionaires' estates of the 1920's and 1930's to survive a 1947 fire. Most recent owner was A. Atwater Kent, inventor. Contains a collection of his early radios.

103

RUGGLES HOUSE, 1818
Columbia Falls
¼ mile off Route 1
Main Street

A two-story Federal house with fanlight and Palladian window, matched boarding on facade, delicate swags over windows. Contains one of the finest flying staircases in New England and remarkable carving on interior woodwork, including rope beading on fireplace cornices. Period furnishings.

BURNHAM TAVERN, 1770
Machias
Corner of Main and Free Streets

A two-story gambrel roof building with early example of running dormer (like Tate House, Portland). Contains Revolutionary War relics.

SOURCES

Society for the Preservation of New England Antiquities (SPNEA). Headquarters—141 Cambridge St., Boston, Mass. 02114. Publishes a booklet describing the properties it owns which are open to the public (25 cents).

The New England Council, 1032 Statler Office Building, Boston, Mass. 02116. Publishes a booklet on houses and museums in all New England states (25 cents).

Maine Publicity Bureau, 3 St. John St., Portland 04102. Distributes a listing on museums and historic houses in Maine, giving dates, hours and admission fees.

Maine League of Historical Societies and Museums, 10 Brann Ave., Lewiston 04240. **Adventures in Maine History,** a bicentennial guidebook to the States historical resources, period houses, etc.

FOR SPECIAL STUDY

Some Good Examples:

Original Paint Colors
Conway House, Camden
Hamilton House, South Berwick
Shaker Village, Poland Spring

Fine Federal Wood Details
Nickels-Sortwell House, Wiscasset
Ruggles House, Columbia Falls
McLellan-Sweat House, Portland

Early Hardware
Parson Fisher House, Blue Hill
Daniel Marrett House, Standish
Parson Smith House, South Windham

18th Century "Cape" Farmhouses
Chapman Hall House, Damariscotta
Conway House, Camden

YOUR ADDITIONAL NOTES

GLOSSARY

anthemion—a flat ornamental design arranged in radiating clusters, usually based on the flowers of the honeysuckle.

balloon frame—a house frame built up from small dimensional sawn lumber nailed together, all walls weight-bearing.

balusters—upright supports of a handrail; in a group a balustrade.

baroque—style in art and architecture developed in Europe from about 1550-1770 and typified by elaborate and ornate scrolls, curves and other symmetrical ornamentation.

batten—a narrow strip of wood, used for flooring.

batten door—a door formed by two or more larger boards held together by smaller boards nailed across them.

bayberry—the wax myrtle, *myrica cerifera,* and its fruit. The coating of wax on the silver gray berries is known as bayberry tallow or myrtle wax and is useful for candle-making.

bed moulding—any moulding below a projecting part.

Bennington knobs—brown mottled ceramic knobs for furniture or doors patterned after those made at the pottery in Bennington, Vt.

blinds—louvered, wooden exterior window shutters.

bolection moulding—a moulding which projects beyond the general surface of a panel or connects two surface levels.

braced frame—a house frame of heavy timbers, usually hewn, supporting floor beams and roof, so that interior walls carry no load. Often pegged and braced at angles. This was the usual method of construction to the mid-nineteenth century. Also called post frame.

Britannia metal—a superior grade of pewter developed in England about 1800 and in the United States in 1825, used for household objects and, after 1840, as a base for electroplated silver.

butt hinge—a hinge composed of two plates attached to abutting surfaces of a door and door jamb and joined by a pin.

candleberry—the fruit of the candleberry or candle-nut tree, *alewrites triloba,* used for making candles.

chamfer—to cut off the edge or corner, to bevel.

chimney breast—the stone or brick structure of the fireplace projecting into a room and containing the flue.

chintzes—bright-colored printed and painted cottons with designs of strange animals, exotic birds, tropical flowers, foliage and vines.

cornice—moulding decorating the junction of wall and ceiling or roof.

cove ceiling—a concave curve where ceiling and wall meet in a room, rather than the traditional right angle.

dado—in interior decoration, the lower part of a wall.

dormer—a window that projects from the slope of a roof.

double-pitched roof—a roof on which one side has two different slopes, as in mansard or gambrel.

ell—an extension of a house, built at right angles to the length of the main building.

embrasure—an opening in a wall for a door or window, slanted so that its interior dimensions are larger than those of its exterior.

espalier—a railing or trellis on which the branches of fruit trees or bushes are trained flat. A plant or row of plants so trained.

fascia board—a flat horizontal band or member between mouldings; especially such a member in a classical entablature.

festoon—a string or garland of leaves, flowers or ribbon, or the like, suspended in a loop or curve between two points.

fireboard—a screen or board used to close off a fireplace when not in use.

fire frame—iron frame set into a fireplace to reduce its size and contain the fire. Uses the brick hearth and sometimes the rear wall of the fireplace.

flue—channel for smoke from fireplace, stove or furnace. One chimney may contain several flues.

flying staircase—a centrally located stairway from one floor to the next with no visible means of support.

frieze—an ornamental band in a building, as on the upper part of a wall.

lath—a narrow, thin strip of wood or metal, used especially to make a supporting structure for plaster, shingles, slates or tiles; or any other building material, such as a sheet of metal mesh, used for similar purposes.

lintel—the horizontal beam that forms the upper member of a window or door frame and supports part of the structure above it.

medium—any solvent with which paint is thinned to the proper consistency.

moreen—a coarse woolen or woolen and cotton fabric, usually watered or embossed.

mortise lock—lock made for insertion in a mortise (cavity) cut into the edge of a door.

myrtle—a bush or small tree of the genus *myrtus* with aromatic berries used for candles, wine and food.

outbuilding—a building separate from, but associated with, a main building.

Palladian window—a three-part window with an arched center section flanked by two smaller side sections. Named after an Italian architect of the 16th century, Andrea Palladio.

panel—a solid piece of wood framed between rails (horizontally) and stiles (vertically) to form a door, wainscot or partition.

patina—a surface mellowing due to age or use.

pediment—the triangular space forming a roof gable or similiar treatment over door or window.

pewter—an alloy of four parts tin and one part lead.

pilaster—a thin, flat column set against a wall, often framing a door or fireplace.

plaster button—a screw with broad, flat washer that is recessed slightly into old plaster, screwed back to the lath and then spackled; used to hold up sagging ceilings.

pleach—to interweave branches, vines, etc. as for a hedge or arbor.

portico—an entrance porch, usually with low-pitched roof supported by slender columns.

quoins—rectangles of stone or wood laid in alternating directions to decorate corners of buildings.

rococco—style of art developed from the baroque that originated in France (about 1720) characterized (in architecture also) by elaborate, profuse designs intended to produce a delicate effect.

sheathing—boards an inch thick or less, often of pine, set vertically or horizontally as walls in early houses; the edges of the boards may be moulded or feathered.

side lights—narrow, vertical windows framing an exterior door.

siding—material, such as boards or shingles, used for surfacing a frame building.

sill—the bottommost horizontal timber of a wall or frame.

size—any of several gelatinous or glutinous substances usually made from glue, wax or clay and used as filler or glaze for porous materials, such as paper, cloth or wall surfaces. Also called "sizing."

smoke bell—a glass bell or dish suspended over a flame, as of a lamp or gaslight, to keep the smoke from blackening the ceiling.

stearine—commercial stearic acid, a mixture of stearic and palmitic acids. (Stearic acid is a white crystalline fatty acid, obtained by saponifying tallow or other hard fats containing stearin.)

summer kitchen—a second kitchen, often built in the ell or wing at a later date than the main house, used for the heavy household chores, particularly involving heat and mess.

"tin"—a type of metal covering made in the form of individual "plates" coated with tin, zinc or alloy. Ceiling often stamped in elaborate patterns.

topiary work—the clipping and trimming of trees and shrubs into regular or unusual shapes.

transom window—a window over an exterior door, made of one row of small lights.

wainscot—the lower three or four feet on an interior wall when lined with paneling or other material differing from the rest of the wall.

winders—wedge-shaped steps used in a winding staircase, also called pie steps.

window sash—a frame in which the panes of the window are set.

wing—an extension of a building with its length parallel to the length of the house.

yew—a slow-growing, long-leaved evergreen of moderate height and spreading habit that lends itself to clipping and trimming.

(Row of roof types in sketches)

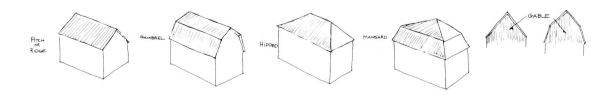

GREATER PORTLAND LANDMARKS, INC., AND ITS RESOURCE CENTER

In 1964, after three important buildings in Portland were demolished, a group of concerned citizens organized Greater Portland Landmarks, Inc. It was an entirely volunteer organization until 1969 when a full-time director was employed. In addition there are now two part-time employees. The office is at 14 Exchange Street in the Old Port Exchange, the restored commercial section of Portland on the water front.

The organization has saved individual buildings in several ways. At first Landmarks became actively involved with the restoration of one house and with the moving of another, both demonstrating dramatically an important part of preservation. More recently a revolving fund has saved many threatened buildings. Houses are bought, covenants are put on them, and then the houses are sold, the money going back into the fund.

Landmarks has made inventories of structures of historical and architectural importance in Portland and has trained groups from surrounding towns to make their own architectural surveys. This is done house by house, street by street. These architectural surveys provide the information needed to identify areas eligible for inclusion in the National Register of Historic Places and are a useful tool for city planners.

"**Portland**", a book on the history and architecture of the city, was written by Landmarks volunteers in 1972. It is now in a second printing. Elwell's **"Portland and Vicinity"**, 1876, was reprinted in 1974 and has sold with great success. A news sheet was started in 1966 and is now a bimonthly publication in newspaper form. It features pictures and articles which keep the membership of over 850 well informed of the many activities of the organization.

Walking and bicycle tours, group tours to other historical centers, an annual open house day in the Portland area, symposiums and a slide lecture series on the history of Portland's architecture are some of the educational events. The workshops of the Advisory Service and its assistance to the owners of old houses are provided without charge.

The Resource Center at Landmarks is a reference library for research for members and non-members. There is room to take notes and browse. It is well stocked with books, journals, bulletins, articles, catalogues, slides and prints on restoration, preservation, architectural history and architectural details. Exhibits of period hardware, fabrics, window hangings and wall hangings are on display. New material is added regularly.

The goal of every preservation group is to educate the citizens of the community to appreciate their architecture and to realize the importance of historic preservation programs in city planning. With better preservation legislation at the Federal and State levels, our architectural heritage will be protected. Hopefully the citizens and the City Fathers will soon be convinced that "the best of the past must be preserved as a living part of the present".*

*Charlton S. Smith, Foreword, **Portland.** Portland, Maine. GPL 1972, p. 8.

RESTORATION ORGANIZATIONS

America Association for State and Local History
1315 Eighth Avenue, South
Nashville, Tennessee 37203

Association for Preservation Technology
1706 Prince of Wales Drive
Ottowa 5, Canada

Historical Mineral Point Inc.
201 Jail Alley
Mineral Point, Wisconsin 53865

National Trust for Historic Preservation
740-748 Jackson Place, N.W.
Washington, D.C. 20006

New York State Historical Association
Cooperstown, New York 13326

Office of Archaeology and Historic Preservation
U.S.D. National Park Service
Washington, D.C. 20240

Old House Journal
199 Berkeley Place
Brooklyn, New York 11217

Old Sturbridge Village
Sturbridge, Massachusetts 01566

Shelburne Museum
Shelburne, Vermont 05482

Society for the Preservation of New England Antiquities
Harrison Gray Otis House
141 Cambridge Street
Boston, Massachusetts 02114